THE HEART
of SELLING

Making Major Sales

TERRY HART

The Heart of Selling: Making Major Sales

This book describes some of the author's experience pioneering a new sales territory. Names and identifying details of individuals and companies have been changed to protect their privacy.

THE HEART
of SELLING

Making Major Sales

TERRY HART

ACKNOWLEDGMENTS

I am grateful to Robert N. Tadross,
my first sales manager and extraordinary sales coach,
to my family, and especially to God almighty,
Who makes all good things possible.

CONTENTS

Prologue

I OPENED THE glass door and entered the lobby with Mike, my friend and colleague. I glanced at my watch as Mike and I approached the receptionist: 3:00 p.m., right on time. We signed the visitor's log as the receptionist decreed. "We're here to see Erica Hildebrand, please," Mike said.

The receptionist barely looked up. "Do you have an appointment?"

"Yes, she is expecting us at three o'clock," responded Mike.

We sat down in the spacious lobby attached to the large set of buildings that housed the manufacturing plant of Elite Products Company, a company that Mike and I hoped would soon become our newest customer. Mike found this prospect in a business directory that listed Erica Hildebrand as the purchasing agent. He had done preliminary sales and marketing research to prepare for my move to Southern California to pioneer a new West Coast sales territory from San Diego to Seattle. Mike was moving to a job based at our company's headquarters that would lead him into executive management. I appreciated Mike's groundwork to justify my new sales territory. He had given me a sizable list of sales leads, which were the fruit of his marketing research. After this introductory meeting with our latest prospect, Mike would be gone and the territory would be mine to grow.

We spoke quietly in the lobby, cognizant that the half dozen people also waiting could easily be some of our many competitors. According to Mike's business directory, this prospect bought large quantities of the types of products manufactured by our company. I hoped to add my first customer to my newborn sales territory.

My excitement over getting this initial sales assignment had grown as Mike and I spent the week scouring the Los Angeles and San Francisco areas in introductory meetings with prospects. Although I had sold a variety of products and services in my youth, this was the first time that a Fortune 50 company had entrusted me with a real sales territory of my own, a company car, a travel and entertainment budget, and, best of all, the freedom to go forth and sell! (Actually, it was not a real sales territory yet. It only had the potential to be developed into one. At the moment, it was primarily a list of prospects.)

"Erica can't see you today." The receptionist didn't even try to sound like she cared.

Mike and I approached the receptionist who seemed to relish the role of gatekeeper. "But we have an appointment," Mike implored. "She is expecting us."

"We have flown here all the way from Houston to see her," I added.

"Sorry, Erica is too busy to meet with you."

We signed out on the register and ignored the glances of others still waiting in the lobby. As we walked to our rental car, Mike swore. "We will never sell anything here. This happened to me last month when I tried to see Erica. You will be wasting your time here. Hopefully some of the other leads will pay off."

Mike and I completed our week of calls on the West Coast. He returned to Texas while I stayed in Southern California. I moved my family out to join me in a rented house so that my wife and I could become better acquainted with the area before buying a home. One of the perks that come with a job in sales is the freedom to live just about anywhere.

I made a phone call to Erica Hildebrand the next month and was surprised when she agreed to meet with me. I told her that I was interested in discussing her needs for the types of products made by my employer. I arrived on the appointed day and time. I smiled at the same stoic receptionist who had turned Mike and me away the previous month. She again pointed me to the sign-in register and muttered something that I could not make out. I signed my name, my company, and noted my time in as 9:00 a.m. "Good morning!" I introduced myself to the gatekeeper. I asked, "What's your name?"

"Leslie. Who are you here to see?"

"I'm glad to meet you, Leslie. I'm here to see Erica Hildebrand."

"Do you have an appointment?"

"Yes I do. She is expecting me at 9:00 a.m."

"Have a seat," Leslie said.

I sat down in one of the corner chairs that gave me a sweeping view of the lobby. There were about ten people already there, seated in several groups. Some appeared to be conducting meetings in the lobby, while others were simply waiting. I was unconsciously developing a sense for quickly sizing up corporate cultures. The feel here was one of efficiency and industriousness. The mood of the room was a little tense but not unhappy. This was a thriving, successful business. I observed the people meeting in the lobby. Some of their faces were familiar as I realized they had been there on my previous visit with Mike.

My thoughts were interrupted a few moments later. Leslie was speaking in my direction without saying my name. "Erica cannot see you today. She is too busy."

"But I have an appointment," I responded.

"Sorry. She is too busy."

As I walked back to my car in the parking lot, I smiled to myself. I still had not even gotten past the gatekeeper receptionist. Arnold Schwarzenegger's character in *The Terminator* came to mind. I could hear him promising in his Austrian accent, "I'll be back." I smiled as I drove to my next appointment.

A month later I was again surprised when Erica took my phone call. I told her that I was still interested in discussing her requirements for the products my company made. She again agreed to meet with me.

When I arrived at Erica's office for the third time, I again smiled at the receptionist, who now had a name. "Hi, Leslie. I'm here to see Erica." I didn't wait to be told to sign in. I again wrote my name and company and noted my time in as 9:00 a.m. Observing that representatives from four of my competitors had also signed the register during the past three days, I made a mental note of their names.

I sat down in the same corner chair and observed the busy lobby. Four people were in animated conversation on the other side of the lobby. I definitely recognized one of them from my previous visits here. He was a young man about my age, late twenties at the time, and was laughing in conversation with the other three. I assumed that he must work here, because he had been here on each of my previous two visits.

A moment later, the door leading from the lobby to the plant offices opened. A woman stood in the doorway holding the door open without actually entering the lobby. She surveyed the people waiting. I stood up and approached her.

"Erica?"

"Yes. You are Terry?"

"Yes, and I'm very pleased to meet you, Erica." I couldn't help but smile.

Erica didn't smile. "What's your price?" She continued to hold the door half open without stepping into the lobby.

No "good morning," no "hello," no "glad to meet you." I tried in vain not to show my surprise at Erica's lack of greeting. How should I respond to her question? My thoughts raced as I remembered my company's training. I had no authority to quote anything but list price until I received approval from my boss to meet a lower competitive price. The only way to get such approval was to tell my boss the name of the competitor, the competing product, and the exact competitive price including delivered freight. The only way to get this information was for the potential new customer to tell me in answer to my questions. I would be embarrassed to quote list price because I knew the price she was currently paying would be significantly lower.

Erica just looked at me with no expression. I heard myself say, "I'm here to offer you the most competitive price—"

Erica cut me off in mid-sentence. "If you can't offer me a lower price than I'm currently paying, then we don't have anything to talk about, do we?" She took a step back and let the door to the lobby swing closed.

I was stunned at what had just transpired. I walked back to the receptionist's window self-consciously and looked at the sign in register for my name: Terry Hart. Sign-in time: 9:00 a.m. I looked at my watch and wrote in my sign-out time: 9:03 a.m. "Where had the time gone?" I mused to myself. I could feel the eyes of everyone in the lobby staring at me. I imagined what they might be thinking about my first interaction with Erica, the purchasing agent. Surely my face was red with embarrassment. I turned around and glanced up. Most people in the lobby looked away and seemed to act as if they had not seen my humiliation. I imagined them thinking to themselves, "Don't stare. Don't make it worse."

One person in the lobby did not look away. He was the young man I had recognized from my previous two visits. He was still in conversation with three other people on the other side of the lobby, but he paused from speaking. I glanced at the name on his company badge clipped to his shirt: Steve Link. He made eye contact with me and smiled. I read the expression on his face and in his eyes. Empathy, not sympathy. I imagined him saying, "Don't give up." I nodded my head.

I exited the lobby and walked to my car, replaying my brief conversation with Erica. Could it be called a conversation? How many words had to be spoken in order to deem it a conversation? What could I have done differently? What outcome had I really expected? Had I considered in advance exactly what outcome I wanted? Surely this was not it.

A year later, a very different scenario existed here. This company became one of my key customers. Erica was placing railcar-sized orders with me. The president of the company knew my name and greeted me warmly whenever he saw me. I counted Erica, the technical director and his staff of researchers, the new business development manager, Leslie the receptionist, and at least five other people here as my friends. What caused this remarkable transformation?

That's what this book is all about: how to understand the selling process and how to apply it gracefully to satisfy customers' needs and make major sales.

Introduction

A SALES DIRECTOR stood in front of one hundred sales representatives and sales managers at his company's annual sales meeting. He peered over reading glasses at his audience and cleared his throat.

"Although growth in our industry is stagnant, we are going to boost our corporation's sales revenue this year by an aggressive 25 percent," he said. "Our corporate directors and I have been meeting for four weeks to devise a sales strategy to accomplish this lofty goal. Our strategy is so simple it's brilliant: we are going to sell more products and services at higher prices."

Sales team members looked at each other in disbelief.

Finally one courageous sales rep spoke up with what everyone else was thinking, "Boss, can't you be a little more specific about how we're going to do this? It would help us if you could offer some practical advice, some detailed strategy, and precise tactics that we could apply to help us sell more products and services at higher prices. What should we do, using the specific talents and abilities that we have, to accomplish this noble goal?"

The Heart of Selling: Making Major Sales answers these questions and more, offering specific, practical, useful, and easy-to-understand advice and principles on how to sell. Going beyond the mechanics of selling, the book first addresses the heart and soul of selling and then the brains of selling in a concise step-by-step approach. With insight and occasional humor, it focuses on a subject that is universally helpful: the ability to sell and to influence people. Not only will this book help you become a truly great sales professional, but it will help you live a more joyful life while making good things happen for your customers.

Years ago I volunteered to participate in a Career Day presentation at my children's elementary and middle school to give the young students a broader picture of potential careers. At the appointed day and time, I stood in the school hallway waiting to give my presentation with about a dozen other parents. The school principal, Sister Theresa, asked each of us what we did for a living. She looked like a wise and caring grandmother and spoke with a lilting Irish accent. Although she was barely five feet tall and conveyed love and warmth, she exuded command and authority as she spoke. I felt like a child who had been called to the principal's office as she slowly made her way around the group of parents.

I listened as other parents answered the principal's questions about their occupations. They included police helicopter pilot, lawyer, CEO, engineer, and software specialist. The man standing next to me was my friend and family doctor. When Sister Theresa approached him and asked what he did for a living, he responded, "I'm a physician."

Sister Theresa gushed, "What a wonderful profession. You're helping people!"

Then she came to me. "And, Mr. Hart, what do you do?"

I was a young salesman then. I would answer this question very differently today. On that day, I just said, "I'm a chemical salesman."

There was dead silence. Sister Theresa's jaw dropped, and I watched the color fade from her face. I could hear her thinking, "Oh, dear Lord, how did we allow this to happen?"

Obviously Sister Theresa's perception of salespeople in general and chemical salesmen in particular was not a positive one. She had undoubtedly encountered some of the salespeople we have all interacted with in our buying experiences, who give the entire selling profession a bad name. (Look on the bright side. Some of these salespeople are our competitors.)

What exactly is a sales representative? What is your role as a sales professional? How do you view yourself and the job you do? The answers depend on whom you ask. Your boss might answer, "Your job is to sell more at higher prices." You might answer, "My job is to represent my company and its products or services to my customers, and to represent my customers to my company." Another salesperson might answer, "My job is to be a problem-solver and valued consultant for my customers." Others might respond, "My job is to manage relationships" or "My role is to develop new business."

Your view of yourself and the job you do is much more important than most people realize. This is because your customers' view of you will simply be a reflection of how you view yourself. Are you a valuable sales professional? Are you a knowledgeable consultant? Do you make people around you happy? Are you trustworthy, honest, and responsive? Do you know how to sell? Would you want to buy from yourself if you were your customer? Your own answers to these questions will shape your customers' answers to these same questions.

PART 1

The Heart of Professional Selling: Customer Relationships

CHAPTER 1

The Importance of
Customer Relationships

SELLING PRODUCTS, SERVICES, and ideas is exciting and rewarding. When you sell by applying the principles described in this book, you can influence people in a positive way to make something good happen for both you and your customers.

Consider the abilities and skills required to succeed in any profession or grand endeavor. It would be difficult to name any single ability more valuable to success than the ability to sell. All truly great leaders, innovators, and world-changers throughout history have possessed remarkable abilities to sell. How else could they have influenced people to embrace their ideas, to try something new, or to "boldly go where no one has gone before?" (*Star Trek* Captain James T. Kirk was a great sales professional.)

Most books and courses on selling focus on mechanics. Many of them use complicated steps, charts, and diagrams to lead would-be sales professionals through hard-to-follow processes and techniques. This book is different.

It begins by addressing the underlying, overwhelming, and sometimes mysterious force that makes truly great selling and influencing possible: relationship. The presence of this positive force brings happiness to all those it surrounds. It causes people to feel fulfilled, joyful, and connected. Why ignore the most important factor in selling?

Relationship is the force and catalyst that enables the selling process to initiate, proceed, and endure. Why is relationship so important to selling?

The selling process usually begins with questions. Relationship allows these needed questions to be asked and answered truthfully, appropriately, and easily. The topic of asking appropriate questions will be covered in depth in part II of this book. At this point, all you need to recognize is that you must ask many good, probing questions in order to be a great sales professional. The best sales professionals ask many more questions than their mediocre competitors. Skilled sales professionals also ask these questions more appropriately and gracefully than their competitors.

As we examine the connection between relationship and the need to ask questions, picture the following scenario. Imagine that you are at an airport waiting to board a flight, leaving on a business trip. A stranger walks up to you and asks the following questions:

- Where are you going?
- How long will you be gone?
- Where do you live?
- Do you have children at home?
- How old are your children?
- What are your children doing while you are gone?
- Who is with your children while you are gone?

Would you answer this stranger's questions? Your mother and I both hope not. What did your mother teach you about talking to strangers? Any prudent person would have serious security concerns about answering such questions from a stranger under these circumstances. You would probably be thinking questions of your own such as:

- Who is this stranger?
- Why is this stranger asking me these personal questions?
- Why does he care how long I will be gone?
- Why is he interested in my children?
- What are his motives?
- Do I need to call the police to ask them to watch my house and my children while I am gone?

Now imagine a slightly different scenario. You are at a PTA meeting at your children's school, a regular gathering in your place of worship, or with some other group you meet with periodically. Someone you do not really know but are certain is part of the group approaches you, smiles, introduces himself to you, and then asks similar questions:

- How old are your children?
- What are they doing this evening?

Would you answer these questions? I suspect that you would answer them without any concern at all.

What is the difference between these two examples that causes you to feel apprehensive and uncomfortable answering questions in the first scenario but completely comfortable answering similar questions in the second? The difference is relationship.

There is no relationship between you and the stranger at the airport, but there is a presumed relationship or connection between you and the stranger at your regular meeting. It is this lack of relationship that prevents you from answering the questions in the first scenario and the presence of a presumed relationship that allows you to answer the questions in the second scenario.

Relationship, or lack thereof, goes even further than simply allowing or preventing answers to flow from questions. Relationship is at the center of interpersonal dynamics in these two scenarios involving strangers asking questions.

How would you regard the stranger at the airport? You would probably be wary and mistrustful of him and feel uncomfortable around him. It is unlikely that you would enjoy the brief conversation with him. If you were to see him again in another airport, you would probably do your best to avoid him. Do you think you would take a phone call from him after this airport exchange?

Why do you think you would regard him with such anxious concern? It is because he asked you inappropriate questions and made you feel uncomfortable. He seemed to be trying to get you to reveal information that you did not want to reveal, at least not to him. This may have even caused you to resent and dislike this stranger.

Without some positive form of relationship, questions necessary in the selling process cannot be successfully asked and answered.

What else can relationship do in the selling process? It can cause a seemingly impossible sale to become possible. Surprisingly, I learned a lesson about this from my daughter when she was in the third grade. She came home from school with another of the endless fund-raiser projects to which modern children are constantly subjected. All students were to sell holiday wrapping paper, with the proceeds going to support the school. I noted proudly that she had already made a list of her prospective customers and saw that her teacher was number one on the list.

I said to my daughter, "You know, it's just not realistic for you to expect your teacher to buy wrapping paper from you. She can't possibly afford to buy from all thirty-five students in your class."

My daughter replied indignantly, "Daddy, I don't want her to buy from all the other kids. I just want her to buy from me!" Words of selling wisdom from a child. We don't want our customers to buy from all those other salespeople. We just want them to buy from us. My daughter came home the next day with an order from her teacher.

Why did she get the order? My daughter felt that she had a special relationship with her teacher. The interest the teacher demonstrated made her feel like her teacher cared about everything in her life. Once my daughter showed the teacher her prospect list with her teacher holding the number one place, it was only natural for my daughter to ask for an order. It was this relationship that overcame odds of 35 to 1.

Relationship is at the center of all major sales, from the very beginning of the selling process. The process never ends. With ongoing business, relationship prevents unpleasant surprises. A solid relationship will lead a customer to tell you when a competitor has offered a lower price on a similar product or service, and the customer will give you the opportunity to meet the competitive price before taking his or her business away.

***

Do you think relationship is valuable only to the seller? Is it worth anything to the buyer for this relationship to be established?

In the past, when one of my family's cars needed repairs, I was in for a time-consuming ordeal. I would usually take the car to three different repair shops, explain the problem at each, and ask for an estimate. Then typically I would leave my car at the shop where I received the lowest estimate.

If I started this *get-three-estimates* process in the morning, it would be afternoon before I settled on where to leave the car. By this time, the repair usually could not be made until the next day. This meant leaving the car overnight.

I was not the only person inconvenienced by this process because it also required that I ask another family member or friend to follow me to the garage to drop off and pick up the car. Usually the car was satisfactorily repaired, but not always. If it still was not right, the process would go on. I would have to leave the car overnight again.

From my (the buyer's) perspective, this get-three-estimates process was too lengthy and filled with uncertainty. Would the repair shop adhere to its first estimate? Would the mechanic tell me he found some other problem that absolutely must be repaired in order to keep my car running safely? Would this previously unnoticed problem double or triple the cost, and was it really necessary?

During one of these three-day repair ordeals, I happened to come across a small, no-frills garage. Its faded yellow-and-blue sign was barely noticeable among a strip of metal buildings in an office/warehouse park. I had to look closely to see that the sign simply read "Kelly's Auto Repair." I parked my Dodge Intrepid – my previous company car – in front and hoped that it would restart when I came back out. I opened the heavy, rusty door to the shop and stepped inside.

There was no receptionist in the small room housing a counter and desk. The walls were adorned with car-racing photographs, trophies, and model cars that seemed to span several decades. I noted the same nucleus of people at various ages in most of the photographs.

I heard the sound of metal on metal coming from the adjacent room. "Hello," I said loudly.

"In here," came the reply. I walked into the room, which was a car-repair stall large enough to work on just one car at a time. A man straightened up from under the hood of a car, and I recognized him from the photographs.

"Kelly?" I inquired.

"Yeah. What can I do for you?" Kelly wiped grease from his hands onto a shop cloth.

I described the Dodge's symptoms. Kelly quickly recited four possible causes, two of which had already been suggested by the dealership I had just visited. I asked Kelly how much it would cost to repair the car. Without consulting any parts lists or manuals, Kelly gave me his estimates to repair each of the four likely problems. He even told me what parts would be required for each repair and that he could have the parts available either today or tomorrow. Kelly's prices were about 20 percent lower than the estimates from his competitors.

I gave Kelly the key to my car and pulled out my cell phone to call my wife for a ride home. Kelly said, "I'll give you a ride."

Riding home in Kelly's pick-up truck, I learned that he started his business many years ago. His son joined him a few years back, and Kelly's wife usually worked in the front office. Car racing was a family passion. So began my car-repair relationship with Kelly and his son.

Car repairs are no longer an ordeal for me and my family. I simply drop my cars off at Kelly's. If it is after normal business hours, I write a note describing my car's problems and slide it under his door, along with my car key. I don't ask what it will cost or when it will be ready. Kelly has my phone numbers. I know he will call me with what he finds, and I'm confident that he will recommend the most economical way to fix or solve whatever problem exists. He won't try to inflate the repair with a string of other unnoticed problems. He will fix it right the first time and charge a fair price. If I cannot get back to pick the car up during business hours, I can pick it up after hours with another key. Kelly knows that I will come by the next day to pay him whatever I owe.

Is this relationship valuable to me as the buyer of car-repair services? Absolutely. Do I miss the agony and inconvenience of the old get-three-estimates process? I don't think so! Do I always get the lowest price? My previous experience gives me the perception that my friend Kelly will charge me a competitive price toward the lower end of the market scale for similar repairs, but I no longer feel the need to test this theory by getting other estimates. I am happy to do business with Kelly. I know that he will repair my family's cars quickly and correctly and stand behind his good work. We know and trust each other.

This relationship gives Kelly all of my car-repair business, and it gives me the convenience of not having to spend several days getting a repair.

***

Anyone who has taken a real estate investment course knows the first three rules of real estate: location, location, location.

Professional selling has its own first three rules: relationship, relationship, relationship.

A great relationship between seller and buyer will overcome a multitude of potential and existing problems, facilitating a mutually satisfying sales transaction and business growth. Conversely, a bad relationship between seller and buyer will allow a multitude of potential problems to become real problems. These will kill most chances for good sales transactions and cause business to shrink. When there is no relationship between seller and buyer, nothing happens.

Early in my sales career, it only took two words from me to make a sale that resulted in more than two million dollars' worth of business over a two-year period. While the buyer and I had enjoyed a superb relationship for many years, he simply did not need anything I sold. As a result, I never gave any thought to selling something to him.

In the course of his business, however, he unexpectedly developed a need for something I sold and called me one morning describing a problem in his manufacturing plant. From his longtime knowledge of the products I sold, he knew that I had a potential solution to his problem.

"Terry," he said, "I need the first truck next week. It will require very specialized fittings. I want to visit the carrier with you to specify what equipment will be needed on the delivery trucks and get them rolling to my plant."

I didn't even have to ask for the order. It was just given to me because I had such a strong relationship with the buyer.

After we hung up, I reflected on this brief phone conversation and realized that we had jumped right through most of the professional selling process and proceeded directly to transaction details for this very large sale. All I did during most of the phone call was listen to the buyer. Then I simply replied with those two powerful words: "Thanks, Dad."

Would you say that I made this sale with relative ability? Contemplating this unusual circumstance reveals much more insight on selling than most people might realize at first glance. Go beyond the surface of a *relative sale* to analyze the significance of what transpired. The Latin root of both relationship and relative is *relatus*. Both words involve a connection between people or things.

Why was this sale so relatively easy? As the seller, why did I not have to call the buyer for many months going through the standard professional selling process? Why did I not have to diligently search for the buyer's need, clarify his problem to him, and present a carefully formulated benefits statement to illustrate how my product was the solution to his problem? Why did I not even have to quote a price?

As the buyer, why did my dad not feel like he had to get three quotes to determine that the price would be competitive? Why was he confident that I would solve his problem?

The one-word answer to all of these questions is relationship.

Obviously we cannot have a father/son relationship with all of our customers, but we can strive to develop relationships that allow our potential buyers to make the same decision my dad made: to buy from us. We can strive to develop relationships that make our customers confident we will do all of the following and more for them:

1) Provide the best solution to their problems.

2) Satisfy their needs most effectively.

3) Offer a price that is competitive or appropriate.

4) Treat them fairly and take good care of them in all aspects of their business.

5) Provide all of the amenities appropriate to the business we are transacting, including technical support, if appropriate;

delivery of products or services according to our agreement and schedule; and all other appropriate capabilities that our company or service has to offer for this type of business.

My dad knew that I would do all of the above for him. He did not feel compelled to check with my competitors. Wouldn't it be nice if every customer felt this way? Why not set this goal for all of our customer relationships? This is not as unrealistic as you might initially think.

CHAPTER SUMMARY

- *Relationship is the force that enables the selling process.*
- *Relationship is required so the questions necessary to the selling process can be asked gracefully and answered truthfully.*
- *Relationship is equally valuable to both buyer and seller.*

CHAPTER 2

Principles for Developing Customer Relationships

THE MOST IMPORTANT requirements for developing superb relationships with your customers come from the heart: genuine empathy, caring, and concern for the people with whom you are interacting. The way you as a sales professional feel toward and treat your customer has a huge influence on how the relationship develops. This doesn't mean only your individual contact but anyone else you encounter at the company you want to sell to: the receptionist (if there is one in this brave new world), the administrative assistant, the technical director, the management, and all those who surround the key decision makers. Empathy is one of the most key ingredients to being a truly great sales professional.

I once attended a business reception in a beautifully decorated hotel ballroom. Everyone in attendance was well dressed in business attire. As I mingled with others, I observed a group of six men and women in conversation. They all greeted each other, smiled, shook

hands, and exchanged pleasantries. They commented on how delicious the food was, how the weather was good for golf, and how they
looked forward to the expected entertainment. However, as soon as
one woman left the group, the remaining five people made condescending comments about her dress and hairstyle. They seemed to
be trying to outdo each other with the harshest criticism, and they
laughed with each added barb.

My impression was that although each member of the group
demonstrated cultured manners while they were all present, it was
obvious that none of them genuinely cared about anyone but themselves. Which of the five would be the next to leave the group and be
subjected to the same mean-spirited criticism? If I, a casual observer,
picked up on this vibe, I thought it likely that each group member
must have sensed the shallow nature of his or her feelings toward the
others.

In selling, there are few things worse than insincerity. Think
about a typical interaction with a telemarketer at dinnertime. Maybe
your caller ID failed, or maybe you were tricked by the phone number displayed. When you answered your phone, how did the last
telemarketer you spoke with try to begin the conversation? He or
she probably asked in an overly excited tone of voice, "How are you
this evening?" Do you think the telemarketer really cared about how
you felt after interrupting your dinner? There are few things worse
than insincere salespeople trying to make you think they care deeply
about you.

It is important to learn from each of our buying experiences
because they provide valuable insight into the selling process. What
did one salesperson do that made you want to buy from her? What
did another salesperson do that made you want to just get away from
him? From my experiences on the receiving end of phone calls from
telemarketers, I no longer greet prospects on the phone by asking,

"How are you?" How many people really want to tell a stranger how they feel over the phone? I would rather be greeted by a simple "hello," followed by a clear identification of the caller and the purpose of the call.

Honesty and Integrity

- Say what you mean.
- Mean what you say.

Wouldn't you rather buy from a salesperson who always tells you the whole truth, never misleads you, and is forthright in all aspects of your relationship? Once a salesperson tells you something that you later learn to be untrue or compromises his or her ethics in some way, how do you feel about future business with this person?

Honesty and integrity are universally respected. They are two of the most valuable traits required to develop and maintain the longstanding business relationships that lead to making major sales. They shine clear, colorful light on a world of gray. Sales professionals who choose every day to walk in this light find that customers will be attracted to them in the long run. Salespeople who choose not to walk in this light find themselves chasing customers in the dark.

Many companies that include honesty and integrity in their mission statements still seem to find it easy to rationalize deviations from the truth. Deviations from a company's published mission statement prevent anyone from taking the statement seriously. The commitment to practicing honesty and integrity must be renewed every day.

Customers have certain expectations coming into any business relationship. It is up to you, the sales professional, to determine what products, services, technical support, and attention your customers need and expect, and to make sure that your organization works to appropriately satisfy these expectations.

It is critical to align your customer's expectations with your company's abilities and desires. If your company separates the products and services it provides into different categories, you must ensure that the organization delivers what is expected for the appropriate category of products and services. You must be your customer's advocate within your company.

CHAPTER SUMMARY

Principles for developing superb customer relationships include:

- *Genuine empathy and caring for people*
- *Honesty and integrity*
- *Appropriate application of resources for the customer*

CHAPTER 3

Obstacles to Developing Customer Relationships

THE TECHNIQUES TAUGHT in some of the misguided sales training regimens of the past are real relationship turnoffs, and these are bad behaviors to be avoided. Most of these behaviors were taught to salespeople in the business of making small sales quickly, without any realistic thought of repeat business with the same customer base. These techniques might still work for quick, low-dollar sales, but they are obstacles to making high-dollar sales and promoting long-term customer relationships.

Have you ever answered your door to an over-enthusiastic person selling magazine subscriptions? These salespeople typically employ a carefully scripted sales pitch riddled with gimmicks, fake sincerity, pleas for sympathy, and manipulation. It's not completely their fault. They are simply following the training they have been given. The approach is significantly different for making ongoing, high-dollar sales from the approach for minor sales such as magazine subscriptions. These low-dollar salespeople get away with this aggressive, in-your-face, gimmicky approach that would get them banned from high-dollar sales.

This gimmicky approach gives the entire sales profession a bad name. Unfortunately but not surprisingly, this is what many people picture when they think of salespeople. Sister Theresa, the grade school principal mentioned in the book's introduction, obviously had this tainted perception in mind when she thought of sales as a potential career for her students. It was not a profession she wanted any of her students exposed to.

Some of the challenges faced by these door-to-door subscription salespeople seem almost insurmountable. They have no relationship with their prospective buyers to begin with, and these prospects probably do not want to deal with them. The sellers probably will never see their buyers again. The sellers probably have less than one minute on average to interact with their buyers. It's a wonder that they ever sell anything. This may be why employers drill desperate gimmicks into these salespeople.

The list of gimmicks employed is trite and tedious. Two of the more common ones are:

- Sympathy. "I can't go home until I sell just one more subscription. Please, Mister, just buy one subscription from me."
- The manipulative line of questions (MLQ). Most everyone has been on the receiving end of this unpleasant experience. The questions are designed to back the customer into a corner. The only way out is to say yes.

Years ago an acquaintance of mine—I'll call him Jack—opened his door to encounter an encyclopedia salesperson. The salesperson quickly launched into the MLQ technique.

"Sir, I can tell that you are a very intelligent man. You must value knowledge a great deal. Would you agree?"

Of course, Jack replied, "Yes." Obviously, answering no would imply that he was not intelligent and did not value knowledge.

"A man who values knowledge will certainly be interested in anything that would increase his wealth of knowledge. Wouldn't you agree?"

Again Jack replied, "Yes."

"If I could show you something that would be a valuable resource to you in your quest to increase your wealth of knowledge, would you be interested?"

"I guess so."

"Well, sir, here it is, a beautiful addition to your wealth of knowledge!" He then enthusiastically presented his set of encyclopedias. "When would you like to add this valuable resource to your wealth of knowledge?"

"But I'm just not sure I want this encyclopedia set. I haven't even looked at any others."

"Sir, this wealth of knowledge comes with a money-back guarantee. You can return it within thirty days for a full refund if you are not satisfied for any reason. You have absolutely no risk. You pay nothing if you don't like it."

"How much does it cost?"

"This valuable addition to your wealth of knowledge is only four hundred and fifty dollars."

Jack replied, "I can't afford that right now."

"But, sir, we have already established that you are an intelligent man and put a high value on knowledge. Isn't this correct?"

"Well, yes."

"Our convenient payment plan allows you to spread your investment in knowledge over a two-year period with no interest charges. Four hundred and fifty dollars over two years comes to just sixty-two cents per day. Sir, are you so poor that you do not have sixty-two cents to invest in your own wealth of knowledge today?"

"Well, no."

"Now that we have established that you do have sixty-two cents per day, you have nothing to prevent you from increasing your wealth of knowledge, do you?"

"I guess not."

"What an intelligent man you are! Sign the order here and your new storehouse of knowledge will arrive in thirty days."

Before Jack even closed his door, he knew he had just bought something he did not really want. Sure enough, a new set of encyclopedias arrived the next month along with a bill for four hundred and fifty dollars plus freight. Without even opening the boxes, he called the phone number on the invoice. "I just received your set of encyclopedias, but I don't want them. How can I send them back for the full money-back guarantee?"

The gruff, male voice on the other end of the line replied, "That's a thirty day guarantee. You have to enjoy them for thirty days before you can send them back."

"But that's not what your salesperson told me. He said they had to be returned within thirty days in order for the guarantee to work."

The voice on the phone responded, "Either he explained it wrong, or maybe you misunderstood. You can't return them yet."

Jack became more suspicious as the conversation progressed. He envisioned being told thirty days later that he had missed the thirty-day window to return the encyclopedias for credit and therefore would have to pay for them.

"Look, I did not want to buy these books," he implored. "Your salesman backed me into a corner with a series of tricky questions. I can't afford these and do not want them."

"Call us back in thirty days, sir."

Jack thought for a moment. "Listen, man, I'm going to prison in one week. I'm trying to settle my affairs before I check in for five years. I can't pay you."

There was a long, quiet pause of surprise on both ends of the phone. Finally, the voice on the other end broke the silence. "OK. Send them back. Here's the address."

Jack was not going to prison. He succumbed to trickery to fight trickery. In his desperation and frustration, he unwittingly followed the bad example set for him in this unpleasant experience. This is not the lesson to learn here.

Consider the actions and methods of this encyclopedia salesperson. He did exactly what he was trained to do. He successfully asked a carefully scripted line of questions designed to get a customer to say yes. There was no real caring or concern for the customer. All he wanted the customer to do was to place the order now. His misguided training did not consider what the customer really cared about or wanted. The one and only goal was to make a quick sale.

Without the benefit of any relationship with the customer, the salesperson made a quick sale with just one sales call to someone who had no intention of buying a set of encyclopedias when he opened his door. This is actually pretty amazing. I imagine his boss was pleased with his performance.

Look at the deceitful and bad result at the end of this true story, however. The salesperson manipulated the customer with a technique to get him to buy something that he did not want. The customer did not pay for the item. He simply returned it. The company incurred two freight charges and made no sale. Both parties lied to each other in the process. What a frustrating mess. Do you think Jack would open his door to this salesperson again? Gimmicks and techniques designed to manipulate customers into buying something they do not want have no place in professional selling.

It is important to note that asking questions is the backbone of the professional selling process. The MLQ technique abuses and misuses the necessary and desired process of asking questions. A misguided salesperson using the MLQ technique seeks only to manipulate the customer into saying yes. A true sales professional asks many effective questions, seeking true answers from the customer's perspective.

Many people will pay a small amount to make gimmicky salespeople go away. For example, they might buy something that costs less than ten dollars just to get rid of this nuisance or maybe because they feel sorry for the person. Do you think anybody would buy something that costs a hundred thousand dollars or more from someone using these techniques just to get rid of them? I don't think so.

How do you really feel when you are on the receiving end of these gimmicks? Do you feel like the salesperson cares at all about you or your needs, respects you or acknowledges that you have a working brain? Do you like being treated like a simpleton when you are on the receiving end of the MLQ technique? Do you think the professional purchasing agents and sophisticated customers you call on will feel any differently?

Professional purchasing agents have taken many training courses, too. They recognize these gimmicks for what they are: desperate attempts to sell something that the buyer does not really want. Gimmicks and trickery have no place in the tool kit for professional selling.

My family and I have enjoyed several vacations in beautiful Cozumel, Mexico. During one of our visits, someone invited us to a luxurious free breakfast at a new resort just a few miles down the beach from our hotel. I felt uncomfortable at the offer of a free breakfast, but my wife, an architect, and I were both interested in the intriguing design of this impressive new structure right on the beach. We accepted the offer.

The breakfast was delicious and filling, including just about every tropical fruit and juice you can imagine, along with savory Central American breakfast dishes. Some of the best coffee in the world was a welcome bonus. As I finished my coffee, this idyllic scene began to change.

An attractive hostess appeared. She didn't speak. She smiled and beckoned us to follow her. She ushered us into another room. It was clear that we were to wait here for someone. Suddenly I remembered a short story I read as a boy, "The Most Dangerous Game" by Richard Connell. This story is about an unwitting traveler who stumbles upon a tropical island and is welcomed lavishly by a mysterious host, only to discover later that his host wants to hunt him like an animal for sport.

We were seated in comfortable chairs at the rear of the room. A large, muscular man in his late forties entered through the only door. Tattoos adorned both of his forearms, and he had the appearance of someone who had spent many years in the sun. He moved a large chair and placed it between us and the door to the room. As he sat in the chair, he looked at us through dull blue eyes. He smiled but conveyed no warmth. He proceeded to tell us about a time-share vacation opportunity that would allow us to return to this resort year after year. At the conclusion of his thirty-minute presentation, he entreated us to invest a large sum of money in this vacation opportunity.

We thanked him for his presentation and for the delicious breakfast but explained that we were not prepared to invest this sum of money in future vacations. We suggested that we might talk again after we had a little time to evaluate the idea.

He shifted in his chair and scooted it a few inches to his right so that he now sat squarely between us and the door. He then suggested that we reconsider. "Why not right now? This opportunity might not be available much longer." His words were polite and his smile remained, but I still felt no warmth. I resolved that the harder he tried to close this sale, the more committed I would be not to buy.

After politely declining three more attempted closings of the sale, we again thanked him for the breakfast and walked around his chair as we left the room.

We can learn so much about selling from our buying experiences. I later considered this free breakfast and time-share presentation in great detail and found much value in the experience. From the moment we were introduced to the time-share presenter, he gave the impression that his goal was to close a high-dollar sale that same morning by intimidating us into making an impulsive decision to buy. He came across as a closer instead of a sales professional. Who wants to be *closed*? I would much rather have a skilled sales professional help me make a joyful, thoughtful decision of my own.

CHAPTER SUMMARY

Skilled sales professionals avoid these obstacles to developing superb relationships in the selling process:

- *Gimmicks*
- *Manipulative techniques*
- *Hard closes to make the sale now*
- *Any pressure to manipulate the customer to do something not in his or her best interest*

CHAPTER 4

How To Develop and Maintain Superb Customer Relationships

IT ISN'T COMPANIES that place orders or make purchasing decisions but the specific people who work for these companies. You cannot really have a relationship with a corporate entity because relationships are between people. This is an important distinction. When people speak of relationships between companies, they really mean the collective relationships that exist between the people who work for these companies.

Most people learned the Golden Rule in kindergarten: Do unto others as you would have them do unto you. This is probably the most succinct advice any of us can ever receive for developing and maintaining relationships of any kind. Its value cannot be overestimated. Other lessons from kindergarten enhance relationships:

- Be responsible.
- Do things well.

- Finish what you start.
- Be on time.
- Do what you say you will.

How do you feel about people who demonstrate the four responsible traits named above? Doesn't if feel good to be able to count on someone, to rely on their words? Why is something so simple becoming so rare?

This simple rule of doing unto others as we would have done to ourselves helps us to demonstrate genuine caring and concern for other people. It allows us to put ourselves in their shoes, to consider their needs and wants before our own.

The title of Robert Fulghum's book is intriguing: *All I Really Need to Know I Learned in Kindergarten*. Most people begin their academic years learning these keys to successful relationships:

- Treat other people kindly.
- Think of other people.
- Share.
- Keep your hands to yourself.
- Don't call people bad names.
- Respect the property of others.

Later in life we seem to be bombarded with opposite messages focused on ourselves instead of others:

- Look out for number one.
- It's all about me and getting my needs met.
- Find myself.
- Get what I want now.

One of the biggest challenges in developing and maintaining healthy relationships is to balance the lessons taught in kindergarten with the lessons taught later in life. Even the Golden Rule requires us to first consider how we would like to be treated ourselves. This contemplation requires that we first know, love, and consider ourselves, but it then looks outward to other people and makes them our focus.

I remember one of the many times an opportunity to apply the Golden Rule snuck past me. I was on a trip to visit customers with my boss, his boss, and another executive. As we approached the Oakland airport in the rental car I was driving, I realized that if I dropped the others off at the terminal first and then returned the car I might miss the flight. I drove straight to the rental car return and turned in the car.

The four of us then carried our luggage through the parking lot and made the long walk to the terminal. As we approached the terminal, the executive traveling with us remarked to me, "Art would have dropped us off right here." Art was a master salesman in our organization and well known for his legendary salesmanship abilities and results. I felt like an inconsiderate heel for not having extended this simple courtesy to my fellow travelers. I resolved to try harder to make thinking of other people first a stronger pattern in my life.

Think of people you enjoy being around. How do they treat you and the other people around them? What is it about their behavior that leads you to enjoy being around them? As I think about the Golden Rule in my sales activities, I recognize that I have opportunities to apply it every day. Most of the opportunities are small, but when added together the sum is big. Little things in life can be big when they help us to form healthy patterns and relationships in our lives.

Another time I was meeting with one of my key customers. During our discussion in her office, I noticed the attractive gold lapel pin she wore. It looked like the emblem communicator featured in the classic television series *Star Trek: The Next Generation.* I smiled and said, "I sure like your pin. In fact, it looks like a Star Trek emblem communicator to me."

She smiled broadly and responded, "You know, I've worn this pin many times during the last few months, and you are the only person who has recognized it for what it really is." This was obviously a minor exchange in our conversation over what most people would consider a trivial matter, but it helped us to make a fun connection that no one else had made before. I had recognized something that was meaningful to her, something she and I both appreciated. You can make big connections by recognizing what is important and significant to your customers.

A short time later, I mailed a book to this customer entitled *All I Really Need to Know I Learned from Watching Star Trek.* I included a brief note explaining that I found the book while browsing in the religion section of a bookstore. I wrote, "Is that appropriate or what?" The next time she spoke with my boss, she began the conversation by asking him, "Has anyone ever told you what a great salesman you have working for you?" She continued to buy 100 percent of her raw materials requirement from our company despite strong influence from her corporate headquarters to buy from one of our competitors.

When you first meet another person, it is natural to look for something you have in common. How many times have you met someone who grew up in a town near your hometown and immediately asked if he or she knew some of the same people you knew in the area?

When you discovered that you did in fact know some of the same people, you probably smiled together at the recognition that you had at least one mutual friend or acquaintance. It is natural for people to feel more comfortable with each other when they discover something they have in common, such as a mutual friend, enjoying the same sport or hobby, or having children of similar ages.

Many people facilitate this search for something in common by surrounding themselves with memorabilia. Potential new customers who decorate their offices with photos and memorabilia of their favorite sport or hobby, family vacations, or alma mater make it easy to begin conversations with kind remarks or questions concerning these mementos. Once on an introductory call with a potential new customer, I recognized a photo on the wall of his office as Mount Whitney, the highest peak in the continental United States. I remarked, "What a beautiful photo. Have you climbed Mount Whitney?"

"Yes. I took that photo on a climb last year." He was obviously pleased. Anyone who has climbed a mountain would be gratified when someone appreciates a photo of the accomplishment.

"I climbed Mount Whitney several years ago myself on a three-day backpacking trip," I said. "The image of the mountain from that vantage point is embedded in my mind!"

I could not help but smile. We then went on to discuss our mutual experiences climbing this mountain. After a five-minute recollection of an adventure that gave both of us pride and joy, we felt comfortable with each other and easily transitioned into discussing our business interests. We were no longer strangers.

Remember the example of the stranger asking questions in the airport? Questions from a stranger make many people feel uncomfortable. When you ask necessary questions of potential new customers, you want them viewing you as a friend, not a stranger.

One of the first things I do each day is work out at my local gym. I follow a carefully planned regimen to train for cardiovascular, strength, and flexibility fitness. While at the gym, I usually see the same group of people at about the same time each morning. I know almost all of them now and we greet each other as we work out. There are still a few people there that I have not yet met or spoken to; the nucleus of the group changes as people's work out schedules evolve over time.

While at a theater in another city about forty miles away, I saw a familiar face from the gym, although this was someone I had never actually spoken to. At the theater we greeted each other warmly and introduced ourselves. Now we are buddies when we see each other at the gym.

Why did we smile and introduce ourselves when we saw each other in an unfamiliar, unexpected place but not when we passed in our daily encounters at the gym? At the gym, we were both simply part of the ambient crowd. At the theater in another city, we stood out from the crowd because we had something in common that the other theater-goers did not. It was this common denominator that made us both feel comfortable initiating an introductory conversation in a different setting.

I have a sticker for Texas A&M University's Association of Former Students on my car. These stickers are so plentiful in Texas that no one seems to notice, but they are very rare on the West Coast. When I came out of church one Sunday after moving to California, I found a note on my windshield from a man I had never met. He noticed the sticker on my car and wanted to introduce himself. The note included the year he had graduated from Texas A&M and a brief background on what led him to California and our church. It concluded with his name and phone number. I called him and was happy to meet another Aggie far from home. Why would someone ignore these plentiful stickers in Texas but go to the trouble of writing an introductory note after seeing the same sticker in an unfamiliar, far-away place? It is human nature to look for things we have in common with each other, especially when we are away from home or in unfamiliar circumstances.

***

Why do people eat breakfast, lunch, or dinner? For many people, the first casual answers might be obvious, even superficially silly. "I'm a little hungry." "I want to try this new restaurant that just opened around the corner." "I need a break from work in the middle of the day, so I eat lunch." "This is my pattern during each day."

Remember the character, Garth, played by Dana Carvey in the *Wayne's World* movies derived from the popular skit on *Saturday Night Live*? Garth was asked by a beautiful woman played by Kim Basinger, "Would you like to have dinner some night?"

Completely missing the point of the beautiful woman's question, Garth responded, "I like to have dinner every night." Me, too.

Consider asking someone in dire circumstances who has not had the opportunity to eat anything in three or four days the basic question of why we eat breakfast, lunch, or dinner. You will probably get much deeper and profound answers. "I want to survive this day." "I want to live." "I want to regain enough energy to care for my family."

All people are just days or weeks away from extinction if too many meals are missed in a row. Most people do not give this fact the slightest thought as they sit down to lunch.

There is something intangibly valuable about sharing a meal with someone. The very essence of this activity is the sustenance of life. Although we do not normally focus our thoughts on this aspect of dining with someone, we are sustaining life together when we share a meal. Under most circumstances, sharing a meal helps us form closer relationships with people.

Many customers are distracted from sales conversations by frequent interruptions in their offices or other work places. Their phones continue to ring. Their coworkers intrude on the sales conversation meeting by coming in to ask questions and get documents signed. Their coworkers may also be observing what is said and done. Customers may feel a subconscious need to impress their coworkers or bosses by being tough on salespeople. For all of these reasons and more, taking a customer out for a meal can be a great way to have an uninterrupted, focused discussion in a relaxed environment. Sales professionals also tend to get more time with customers in a restaurant than they do in their offices.

You should not make it standard practice to invite potential new customers to a meal for the initial meeting. Skilled sales professionals take the opportunity to meet with a new customer first in a normal business setting. This gives you the opportunity to ensure that the prospect truly has the potential to be a decision-making new customer. It allows you to overcome the stranger persona. As you find out more about this person and what is important to him or her, potential topics appropriate for conversation during a meal may surface.

Lunch is frequently a more appropriate backdrop for business discussions than either breakfast or dinner, but this depends on the customer's circumstances. Most cities and towns have their power-lunch locations, where many people vie for the best tables to be seen *doing lunch* with each other. In most circumstances, picking one of these hot-spot lunch locations would only be important if it is important to the customer. Otherwise, a relatively quiet restaurant with good food and attentive service is the most helpful place to conduct sales conversations.

Many customers with families tend to avoid dinner meetings because their time spent at home with their loved ones is already limited by heavy work schedules and business travel. If you invite customers to meet for dinner, it is thoughtful to include spouses when possible or appropriate.

Time is precious. Before scheduling a sales call with a potential new customer, you should make sure that the customer could conceivably use the product or service you are selling. Savvy sales professionals don't waste either party's time calling on people who have no potential to become customers. This seems obvious, but sales professionals in a hurry or under pressure to make a specific number of calls may be tempted to take shortcuts that are costly both to themselves and their prospective new customers.

The Internet makes qualifying customers in advance much easier than it used to be. Most other aspects of professional selling are more challenging today because of competing priorities, busier schedules, fewer people doing more work, and multiple initiatives forced upon purchasers and salespeople alike that inadvertently distract from sales and purchasing excellence.

Most companies put tremendous amounts of worthwhile information on their own websites. By simply accessing a company's site, you can gain valuable insight into a potential new customer and find answers to many of your background questions. What products does the company make or what services does it provide? What industries does it serve? What are the company's current objectives and initiatives? What is its financial condition? Could this company be a credit risk? How big is the company, and how many employees does it have? Where does the company operate? Who should be the initial point of contact?

In years past, many sales professionals used expensive business directories to find this type of background information. Directories can still be very helpful, but the Internet is an amazing resource.

When a potential new customer is found, it is very helpful to get the name and phone number of the purchasing decision maker. When calling to schedule an initial appointment, asking to speak with a specific person makes it much easier to connect than asking for an unnamed purchasing agent. A friendly receptionist might answer questions as to who buys the product or service in question within the organization, but many companies no longer even have receptionists to ask.

Once you identify decision makers for the product or service being sold, call and ask a few clarifying and qualifying questions. It is up to you to convince the prospective new customer that it will be worth his or her time to meet for the initial discussion.

Call Plans

As with most relationships, regular contact is required to develop and maintain customer relationships. How frequent should this contact be? In the initial stages of developing a customer relationship, meeting at least once per month or even every three weeks is helpful. Be sure you have something meaningful to discuss or present each time. You must bring value to the customer in each meeting so he or she can justify the time invested with you.

A written call plan is an effective sales tool to ensure that you develop and maintain relationships with specific people through regular contact. Although a call plan seems so easy to write and is obviously effective, a surprising number of salespeople fail to use this valuable tool, making it difficult to adhere to very-necessary regular contact. Without regular contact, customers forget who you are and relationships grow stale. Sales professionals who operate without call plans frequently see their efforts degenerate into pinball mode, reacting to their environment like a pinball bouncing off paddles instead of proactively planning and executing their sales plans.

Think about the people you have met recently. Do you remember their names and faces? Do you remember which companies they work for, what their job titles are, and what interests them? If you have only met them once, you are unlikely to successfully answer these questions. For people you have met with many times, most likely you will easily answer these questions several months later.

What about someone you previously met with but have not seen in more than a year? Will you remember the answers to these questions regarding that person? That probably depends on how close your relationship was before.

Spreadsheets are an excellent format for call plans. Following is an example of the types of information to include in column headings on a spreadsheet-based call plan:

Person's Name	Company Name	Person's Title	Location (City, State)	# of Calls Planned Per Year	Dates of Calls Actually Made
				(This focuses	(This could be 12
				on call	columns with Jan.-Dec.
				frequency)	headings used to
					ensure that the Call
					Plan is being followed.)

Include any additional information you think will assist you. The plan can be sorted using the spreadsheet tool in a variety of ways.

Note that it is especially important to include the column heading "Location" so that travel to meet with customers can be planned efficiently. The call plan also requires that you identify the specific key decision makers within your customers' organizations. This list of key decision makers will probably change frequently, so it is important to update the call plan periodically as needed.

Polite persistence is required to follow the call plan. Customer visits will not always be easy to schedule, even with existing customers. This is especially true today when most people are doing jobs previously done by several people. Over-scheduling is the plague of our time.

Recognize that difficult customers can sometimes be the most loyal of customers. If the potential is great for business with a difficult customer, remember that once you have established a relationship with this person, the customer is likely to stiff-arm your competitors as hard as he or she stiff-armed you in the beginning.

Another helpful tool to build effective customer relationships is to entertain your customers with events of specific interest to them. When entertaining, it is important for you to host the customer instead of simply giving away tickets to an event. The objective is to develop a relationship. How can you develop a relationship with the other person if you are absent? Imagine a couple going out on a first date. Imagine the person who extended the invitation giving his or her date one ticket to a movie and then waving goodbye to the date as the date enters the theater alone or with someone else. Do you really think the movie-goer will think fondly of the absent date just because he or she provided a ticket to the movie without sharing the experience?

***

A number of few years ago, my family and I wanted to build a swimming pool in our backyard. We didn't know anyone in the swimming pool construction business, so we did some research to find three companies from which to request proposals. All three responded, visited the site, and offered proposals and designs. After careful consideration, we picked the company that appeared to have the potential to do the best job.

We were excited when a work crew arrived with a small Bobcat earthmover and began digging a hole in the yard. After a day and a half of digging, the hole was complete. As the digging crew left, rain began falling. It rained nonstop for three days, and the ground became saturated with water. When the rain finally stopped, I stood in the yard surveying the hole that was to become our pool, now partially filled with muddy water. As I looked at the mud from ten yards away, the saturated ground gave way in the deep end. The hole collapsed and disappeared into the mud. It now looked like an undefined mess.

I called Martha, the construction coordinator who was my primary contact at the pool company we had hired, and reported what had happened. She sounded concerned and told me she would have Barry, the construction superintendent, call me.

Several days went by and nothing happened. I called the pool company to check the status. A receptionist answered and I said, "Could I speak to Martha, please?"

"She is not available. Could I take a message for her?" I left a message asking Martha to call me back. She did not call. The next day I called again with the same result.

The following day I called and asked for Barry, the construction superintendent. The receptionist replied, "He is out on a job. Can I take a message?"

I again explained my concern over the muddy pit in my yard and asked how this problem could be fixed. The receptionist assured me that someone would call back. Again nothing happened. I began to think that we had made a big mistake. We had hired the wrong company to build our pool. If I had the decision to make over again, I definitely would have chosen a different company to build the pool. I reread our contract and focused on the cancellation clause.

Early the next morning, I finally received a phone call from Martha, the construction coordinator. "Mr. Hart," she said, "I just wanted to let you know what we have been doing behind the scenes on your job. I know you probably think we haven't been doing anything, but that's not the case. Our guys will be at your house later this morning. We have a carpentry crew lined up to build a wooden form around the deep end of your pool to make the size and shape conform to the original plan. Another crew will follow to immediately fill dirt behind the form. The steel crew will be there tomorrow to install the rebar, and the gunite crew will be there the very next day to spray the gunite."

This phone call completely changed my perception of the pool company I had hired. The company completed the pool construction in fine form.

Salespeople seriously damage their reputations and customer relationships when they fail to respond promptly to phone calls or any forms of communication from customers. It is especially damaging when sales professionals fail to respond to concerns expressed by customers or fail to communicate effectively with customers when problems arise.

Think of your own buying experiences to reinforce this point. How do you feel when a salesperson does not return your phone calls? Doesn't this make you want to buy from someone else? Many salespeople seem to disappear when problems arise. Nobody wants to communicate negative information, but this is not the time to hide. If Martha had promptly responded to my first phone call expressing concern over the cave-in, my relationship with the pool company would not have been damaged. If she or someone else in the company had simply communicated to me what planning and steps were being taken behind the scenes to correct the cave-in problem, I would not have been concerned in the least. Their failure to communicate was a much more serious business problem than the cave-in of the hole.

When things go wrong and problems arise, frequent and accurate communication with your customers is essential to preserve and strengthen your relationships. Once problems are resolved, your relationships with customers can actually be stronger than before. You will be viewed as a reliable supplier who will not disappear when times are tough.

Practicing these simple courtesies will distinguish you from much of your competition:

- Return phone calls promptly.
- Execute follow-up plans responsively.
- Do what you say you will do when you say you will do it.
- Carefully consider situations before making commitments.
- Plan to under-promise and over-deliver on commitments.
- Communicate; don't leave them hanging.

Skilled sales professionals make these simple courtesies high-priority patterns in the way they do business with their customers. Their relationships are enhanced significantly as a result.

Let your customers know that you are thinking of them and have their interests in mind. Simple actions and gestures are meaningful. For example, when you come across a newspaper article on a topic of interest to one of your customers, send him or her the article with a short note saying, "I thought of you as I read this article and knew you might be interested." Sending articles is easier today than ever when they can be forwarded via e-mail as long as copyright laws are followed. Many newspapers facilitate the electronic forwarding of articles with appropriate acknowledgements.

Be attentive to all things important to your customers. I know a high-performing sales professional who makes a habit of bringing something of nominal cost but high value to customers on most calls. He zeroes in on things that are obviously of specific interest to each individual with whom he interacts, including executive administrative assistants, receptionists, and other people who many times control access to key decision makers. His phone calls are usually answered promptly.

Relationship is the heart of the selling process. Everything else pales in comparison to the value of relationship. Skilled sales professionals recognize that a great relationship will allow them to correct many shortcomings. A bad relationship will create insurmountable problems.

People want to do business with people they know, trust, and like. If a relationship is solid, most customers will help sales professionals solve problems to allow sales to take place. For example, they will call if a competitive situation arises and give the sales professional the opportunity to address it.

Best-selling author Rick Warren said it well in his book *The Purpose Driven Life*:

"In our final moments we all realize that relationships are what life is all about. Wisdom is learning that truth sooner rather than later. Don't wait until you're on your deathbed to figure out that nothing matters more."

CHAPTER SUMMARY

How to develop and maintain effective sales relationships:

- *Remember that specific people are your customers; companies are simply the employers of your customers.*
- *Apply the Golden Rule...always.*
- *Focus on what is important to your customer.*
- *Look for common denominators to build rapport.*
- *Meet with customers for meals whenever possible.*
- *Qualify prospective new customers before contacting them; don't waste either party's time.*
- *Once initial contact is made, sustain it with follow-up visits by using a written call plan.*
- *Be responsive...always.*
- *Understand that relationships with customers are more valuable than any order or any other aspect of business.*

PART II

A Practical Process To Make Major Sales

A professor is someone who can take something simple and make it complicated. A communicator is someone who can take something complicated and make it simple.

—Dr. Barry Asmus

CHAPTER 5

Overview of the Selling Process

THE SELLING PROCESS comprises three phases:

1) **Ask** questions to discover and develop the customer's needs, problems, opportunities, or wants.
2) Present **Benefits** of your product or service as the solution.
3) Gain **Commitment** from the customer to make major sales.

Ask, Benefits, and Commitment are the ABCs of the professional selling process, and relationship is the foundation for the entire process. Like most processes, each phase must be completed in proper sequence, with phases 2 and 3 relying on work done in the prior phase.

After reading many books, taking a wide variety of courses, and listening to countless presentations on the subject of selling, I continue to be dumbfounded at how unnecessarily complex many courses try to make this subject. Authors and presenters use a misguided stream

of complicated charts, diagrams, and forms to guide sales professionals through a process that only becomes convoluted and lost in minu-
tia. This burdens sales professionals with nonessential baggage that
hinders their effectiveness in sales discussions with customers.

During the early years of my sales career, I used to take everything I thought I might possibly need on business trips. Perspiration
flowed even in cold weather as I lugged large, heavy suit-cases and
thick binders filled with data, product literature, samples, and presentations through endless airports, onto rental car shuttles, and into
hotels. When I needed something quickly, I had to search through all
this stuff to get to it.

Watching myself and other salespeople bag-dive during sales
calls—rummaging through overstuffed briefcases for some piece of
information to show to a customer—helped me realize that life is
much more pleasant when we focus on what is truly needed. I began
to travel light and only brought what was useful. When something
was needed, I could quickly and smoothly produce it because I did
not have to sift through unnecessary clutter to get to it. The difference in these approaches is the difference between being Inspector
Clouseau and being James Bond. Clouseau is funny and I like him,
but Bond sells a lot more movie tickets.

Let's cut through the clutter and focus on the truly effective
essentials of professional selling.

CHAPTER SUMMARY

The ABCs of the professional selling skills process are:

Ask: *Ask questions directed toward discovering the customer's needs, problems, opportunities, or wants.*

Benefits: *Present the benefits of your product or service as the answer to the needs, problems, opportunities, or wants expressed by the customer.*

Commitment: *Get an appropriate commitment from the customer.*

CHAPTER 6

Ask

ASKING QUESTIONS IS the backbone of the professional selling process. Establishing a good, solid business relationship with your customer is the heart of the process and should remain your underlying focus. Once the relationship is established, at least on an introductory level, the Ask phase can successfully proceed.

The objective of the Ask phase is to discover your customer's needs, problems, opportunities, or wants, which I refer to as Need POW™. Your customer's Need POW is the door to making sales. Find the door by appropriately asking the right questions. Open the door by presenting benefits of your product or service as the solution to Need POW. Walk through the sales door with a commitment from the customer.

No one buys a product or service unless it meets a specific need, solves a particular problem, allows the person to take advantage of an opportunity, or simply satisfies a want. This is why successful sales professionals begin the selling process by focusing on customers' needs, problems, opportunities, and wants. This search for Need POW requires the sales professional to ask questions, which can be a fun process when you first establish a good relationship. It requires the skills of a detective combined with genuine caring and empathy for the customer. Imagine going to a doctor, signing in with the doctor's receptionist right on time for your appointment, and taking a seat in the waiting room. Thirty minutes go by. Forty-five minutes crawl by. Finally, after you have waited for an hour, a nurse calls your name. You stand up expectantly and follow the nurse into an exam room. The nurse tells you that the doctor will be in to see you soon and closes the door as she leaves.

You look at the doctor's diploma and credentials on the wall as you continue to wait. Twenty more minutes escape from your life. Thirty more minutes go by. You think of all the work piling up in your office. You wonder if you are feeling better now. Is it worth waiting? You think about leaving.

You start to play with the medical instruments and tools hanging on the wall. Suddenly you hear a quick knock on the door. You scramble to put all the medical exam tools back where you found them. A doctor in a white coat walks in briskly. He doesn't look directly at you. He glances at the chart in his hand. He says your name as he peruses the information very briefly.

The doctor says to you, "I just returned last week from a medical conference in San Diego. I learned a new and improved surgical technique that you are going to love! Patients recover much faster from this new surgery than they did from the older version I previously used. You will only be hospitalized for five days and then recuperate for two short weeks at home. You can return to work just three weeks after your surgery. Isn't that amazing? I will also prescribe some new drugs for you. You are going to love these medications. The side effects are not *that* bothersome. I'm going to schedule you for surgery on Tuesday of next week. Be at the hospital no later than 7:00 a.m. Don't eat anything after midnight the night before."

He immediately starts scribbling prescriptions on a pad and hands them to you. He then exits the room as quickly as he entered without even noticing the astonished look on your face.

Would you show up for this new and improved surgery on Tuesday? Would you ever come to see this doctor again? I certainly hope not. He has not bothered to diagnose your medical problem; but he has already scheduled you for some unknown surgery and written prescriptions for mystery medications with no knowledge, care, or concern for what really ails you. No prudent person would ever seek medical help from a doctor who offered surgery and drugs without trying to diagnose a medical problem first.

As preposterous as this story sounds, many salespeople behave like this doctor when they try to sell something to a customer without first taking the time to find out what the customer really wants. Think of your own buying experiences. How many times have you had a salesperson quickly and bluntly present what he or she assumes are the benefits of a product or service to you without first asking appropriate questions to determine what you really want? Don't you find this type of presumptuous behavior annoying?

Imagine pouring newly discovered crude oil into the gas tank of your car. What do you think would happen? Nothing good. Before crude oil can be used as fuel, it must be refined into useful gasoline, diesel, or jet fuel. This is what talented salespeople do after they discover a problem or want. They refine it into something much more useful to the customer and to themselves.

Once you discover your customer's specific problem, develop it with further questions that encourage the customer to consider deeper aspects of the problem that may not have occurred to him or her before. How significant is this problem or need? What does it mean to your customer? Does your customer face this problem every day? What are the implications? What does this problem cause him or her to do or not do? Encourage your customer to quantify the value or cost of the specific problem if he or she is unable to take advantage of the available opportunities to fix it?

These questions expand the meaning of your customer's need, allowing it to ripen and mature. They encourage a call to action on the part of your customer. Development of needs can be thought of in terms of the following word picture:

DEVELOPMENT OF NEED POW

Everything is perfect

Maybe things could be better

This is actually a problem

I need to change this sometime

I WANT TO ACT ON THIS NOW!

Let's face it. Most of the time when sales professionals find a qualified prospect who buys the type of product or service being offered, the prospective new customer will make statements such as these:

"I do not really have a need for another supplier of this product."

"I already have a provider of a similar service."

"I already have good suppliers. I do not need another one."

"Nothing is broken. Nothing needs fixing."

The implied message is usually "I don't need you. Now go away." This scenario is reminiscent of the true story in the prologue of this book. This is precisely why continuing to ask broader and deeper questions in an appropriate way during sales conversations is the key to first discovering and then developing needs. This is what drives the sales conversation from the search for needs to "I want to buy from you now."

The most successful sales professionals ask many more questions than their average counterparts. This desire and ability to ask the right questions appropriately can be easily observed in their sales conversations with customers.

Consider what great sales professionals might ask for if they were granted three wishes:

1) My customers' permission to ask an unlimited number of questions.

2) Completely honest and open answers from my customers.

3) The ability to really listen to my customers' answers.

Having these three wishes come true would always give you the information needed to offer the right benefits and connect your product or service to your customer's problem or need. This would lead to closing the sale with an appropriate commitment.

Asking questions drives this entire process. Salespeople who conduct sales conversations primarily by making statements sell far less successfully than great sales professionals who focus their conversations on asking questions and listening insightfully to customer answers. The key is to ask and listen.

To be a great sales professional, don't tell your customers what to do. Let your customers tell you what they need and describe their problems to you. Let your customers picture and expound on the opportunities they have to solve their problems. Then encourage your customers to act on their needs and to count on you to fulfill those needs.

Deeper questions require deeper, closer relationships to get real answers. Again, remember the airport questioner story from chapter 1. You will very likely need to call on a customer a number of times to develop a stronger relationship before you can expect to get all the answers needed to make major sales.

These are common mistakes made by many salespeople:

1) Not asking enough questions
2) Not asking appropriate follow-up questions to clarify the meaning of previous answers given
3) Not developing the implications of Need POW with deeper questions
4) Not quantifying or clearly exposing the implications, meaning, and value of Need POW
5) Not asking questions to encourage action
6) Telling customers what to do, instead of helping customers to reach their own conclusions based on their own answers to insightful, appropriate questions

Even though most sales professionals fall into the category of not asking enough questions, some salespeople also alienate customers during the Ask phase by asking too many questions or by asking them in an inappropriate manner.

How do you feel when someone asks you a seemingly endless list of questions? Do you enjoy being interrogated? Do you want a stranger to pry into the deepest yearnings of your life? Do you think your customer will feel any differently than you do about being questioned?

In an introductory meeting with a new purchasing agent, I was intrigued by her unique business background and began asking her questions about things she had done in her previous jobs. I was truly interested. However, after about ten minutes, she said she felt like she was on the old TV game show *This Is Your Life*. I was embarrassed. I realized that I had inadvertently crossed the line from showing sincere interest to making her feel uncomfortable with too many questions.

Ask questions using a conversational tone, not as if you are conducting an interrogation. Be careful not to make customers feel threatened. Avoid putting customers on the spot with potentially controversial questions, especially in front of their bosses or coworkers.

Usually you will get more revealing answers in a one-on-one sales conversation because the presence of the customer's boss or coworkers will affect his or her answers. In the presence of a boss and coworkers, your customer may be thinking "What will the others think of my answer?" or "What can I say to make my coworkers think I am really tough on salespeople?" or "Will my boss think I am giving away too much information?"

There are obviously times when it is appropriate to include a larger number of other people in sales conversations, but when you need answers to deep questions, it is best to meet one-on-one with your customer.

Consider when it is appropriate to take notes as you listen to your customer's answers to questions. Depending on the topic, the customer may be hesitant or reserved if he or she feels the answers are being recorded. On other occasions, your customer may feel somewhat demeaned if you do not take notes. If the answers involve details, numbers, and complexities, it is best to write them down. While taking notes, be sensitive to any change in tone or manner from your customer that could indicate the person may not speak as freely if notes are taken.

Establish a pattern of questions that build on each other to first reveal and then develop and refine your customer's Need POW. Asking questions can be like surfing. The surfer knows he wants to catch the wave, stand up, and ride it with style; but the way the wave breaks determines which direction he should go and what maneuvers he can perform as he rides it. Similarly, the way sales conversations flow determines how questions should be asked and what questions should be asked.

CHAPTER SUMMARY

The objective in the Ask phase is to discover the customer's needs, problems, opportunities, or wants. Once discovered, these needs are developed with further questions to:

- *Emphasize their reality and significance*
- *Quantify their implications and meaning to the customer*
- *Encourage a call to action*

Sales professionals carefully listen to their customers' answers to determine:

- *What questions to ask next*
- *How to ask the questions*
- *When to present benefits*
- *What benefits to present*
- *What commitment to ask for*
- *When to close or ask for commitment*

CHAPTER 7

Types of Questions

THERE ARE TWO primary categories of questions used during the Ask phase. They are background questions and Need POW questions.

Background questions simply examine the customer's situation. They seek a description of the customer's circumstances. They ask for revelation and elaboration on the world in which the customer lives, works, and operates. Background questions and their subsequent answers help you to formulate and ask the more important and revealing Need POW questions.

Use Need POW questions to first discover your customer's needs, problems, opportunities, and wants, then to examine the implications of these needs to your customer. For example, what does the need or problem really mean to your customer?

Once a problem is uncovered, use Need POW questions to quantify its significance and importance. These questions delve into true meaning and perspective. They encourage a call to action.

Both types of questions are important. Background questions are the foundation for Need POW questions. It is interesting to note that background questions frequently are easier to ask and are more obvious in nature. They can appear somewhat superficial or even mundane. They are asked more often and require less thought and less insight to ask and to answer. Although relationship is always key and at the heart of the selling process, background questions require a lower level of relationship to ask and answer than do Need POW questions.

Background Questions

Remember the old *Dragnet* TV show? In this classic police detective series, Sergeant Joe Friday frequently said, "Just the facts, ma'am." He would try to keep the people he was questioning on track with this phrase. He did not want speculation or irrelevant chitchat, just the facts. Background questions tend to focus on the facts. Examples of common background questions include:

- What do you buy?
- How much do you buy?
- Who are your current suppliers?
- What price do you currently pay?
- How long have you been in business?
- How long have you been at this location?
- What were your gross sales last year?
- How many people work here?
- Who is the primary decision maker for this purchase?
- Where are your manufacturing plants?

Observations and Concerns with Background Questions

Skilled sales professionals recognize that the questions they ask and the manner in which they ask them affect their relationships with customers. They realize that every salesperson who calls on their customers is probably asking similar background questions.

Put yourself in your customer's shoes. If your customer already met with eight other salespeople earlier in the day, you don't want to be the ninth person to ask "What do you buy?" Purchasing agents get tired of answering the same old questions day in and day out. Try to make you customer's life more interesting and meaningful during sales conversations. This makes you more valuable and memorable to your customer than your average competitors.

At an air show my family attended years ago, there were many high-performance and even exotic-looking airplanes on display. The F-18 Hornet was just being rolled out to the Navy and Marines, and this was the first time I had seen one up close. As I marveled at the jet, I had a pleasant conversation with the proud pilot standing next to his plane. When the air show was over, my wife and I invited the pilot to dinner. At the end of our dinner, we exchanged addresses and phone numbers as we were leaving the restaurant. Without giving it much thought, I then asked him, "How fast will you fly your F-18 as you return home?"

He replied, "That's question number 399." From the tone of his voice and the expression on his face, I sensed that he was a little bit disappointed by my question. He had obviously been asked this question and many others by the huge crowd of people who attended the air show. This question might have made him feel that I was more interested in his airplane than in him.

Skilled sales professionals understand that the questions they ask and how they ask them definitely affect their relationships with customers. It is important to balance the need for information with the deeper need for good relationships.

Minimize the number of background questions you have to ask by researching the customer's website or other sources before the sales call. Anything you can learn in advance helps you minimize the need for background questions so you can maximize the time spent with your customer and focus on more productive Need POW questions.

Remember that you can only ask a finite number of questions during the precious time you have with your customers, and answers to background questions just provide background information. Answers to Need POW questions lead to making major sales. It is more beneficial both to you and to your customers if the majority of this time focuses on the more fruitful Need POW questions.

Need POW Questions

As you learned in the previous chapter, Need POW questions are asked to reveal and develop a customer's needs, problems, opportunities, and wants. These questions go deeper than background questions. This is where the real heavy lifting is done in the selling process.

Most people think of selling as delivering a smooth, convincing sales pitch that leads customers to buy. This is not an accurate picture of professional selling. The genuine backbone of selling is the process of asking insightful, thought-provoking questions in an easygoing, non-threatening, conversational manner to discover what customers really want or need. This is the most challenging part of the selling process.

Think about it. To be a successful sales professional, you need the quick wit of a superb and caring talk show host to engage the customer in an interesting conversation. You need the insight of a wise sage to connect ideas that your customer may not have considered to be related. You need the empathy of a saint to sincerely listen, feel, recognize, and care about what your customer cares about.

Why do people purchase anything? They need something to survive, such as water, food, shelter, health care, or security. They have a problem that must be solved, such as a leaking pipe causing water damage. They have an opportunity to do something appealing, such as buying a house with an affordable mortgage interest rate. They want something to make their lives better, such as education, comfort, style, or efficiency.

Think of your own buying experiences. How many times have you walked into a store to buy something when you didn't have any needs, problems, opportunities, or wants? If you went shopping as a form of entertainment without having a specific shopping list, you wanted entertainment. Most people probably would not walk into a store unless they were fulfilling a need, solving a problem, pursuing an opportunity, or satisfying a want. Most people do not buy because a salesperson delivers a smooth sales pitch. They buy to satisfy their Need POW.

Open and Closed Questions

Both background questions and Need POW questions can be either open or closed. Closed questions usually require only a one-word answer such as yes or no. Closed questions are typically used as background questions or in a series of questions to set the stage for more revealing questions. An example of a closed question is "Does your company own this building?" This question requires a simple yes or no response.

Open questions usually require more thought to ask and to answer. They are typically more revealing and engaging in conversation. Many times open questions begin with how or why. They focus on implications and insights. An example of an open question as a variation of the previous closed question example would be "How do you decide whether to buy a building or to simply lease office space?" This question cannot be answered with a simple yes or no. Its answer will reveal more insight into the customer's operation than the previous closed-question example. However, the closed question might have been necessary to determine what open question to ask.

For example, if the answer to the closed question had been no, then the follow-up open question might have been different. The open question could more easily lead to an insightful and engaging conversation. Both open and closed questions are useful, but you should focus on open questions to maximize the exchange of information and to energize the sales conversation.

Develop Needs, Problems, Opportunities, and Wants with Further Questions

You know you are achieving success when customers answer your questions or make statements that begin with phrases such as:

- It would be nice if we had...
- Yes, that really is a problem when...
- We could pursue this opportunity if we only had...
- We need...
- I want...

When you hear answers such as these, you can ask Need POW development questions to help quantify, explain, and expand the implications and meaning to the customer. Need POW development questions that could be used as follow-ups to the above answers might include:

- What would it mean to you if you had…?
- How much does it cost you when this problem occurs?
- What would this opportunity mean to you and your organization?
- How does it hurt your organization when you do not have what you need?
- What would it mean to you to have exactly what you want?

An Expressed Need POW Is the Only Real Need POW

Understand that it is important for a customer to actually express his or her needs in answer to your questions. If this is not what your customer is doing, then you cannot be certain the customer knows or fully recognizes the want or need. The only way for you and your customer to be certain of a specific need is for the customer to clearly say what it is.

How many people truly know what they really want? Much of the value sales professionals bring to their customers is the ability to help them discover what they really need and to understand the implications of what this means to the customer.

CHAPTER SUMMARY

The two primary types of questions in the selling process are background questions and Need POW questions. Background questions simply examine the customer's situation and tend to be factual in nature. They are the foundation for Need POW questions, which search for customer's needs, problems, opportunities, or wants and then develop their implications. Both types of questions can be open or closed, although the most helpful Need POW questions are usually open questions.

CHAPTER 8

How To Ask Questions

I LOOKED AT my caller ID as the telephone rang at home one Saturday afternoon but did not recognize the caller's name because it was truncated on the display. I thought it might be a friend, so I picked up the phone and was immediately surprised not to hear a friend's voice. The caller was a stock broker making cold calls to prospect for new clients.

Many tasks still loomed on my Saturday to-do list, so I was not interested in spending fifteen minutes answering personal questions asked by a stranger. I empathized with a fellow sales professional working to make a living for his family, however, so I listened for a moment. I appreciated the fact that he did not begin by asking, "Mr. Hart, how are you this afternoon?" When a stranger begins a phone conversation with this insincere question, I immediately wonder what they are going to try to sell me.

In this case, the caller clearly identified himself and told me why he was calling. This relieved the apprehension that most people feel when they answer their home phone and hear a stranger's voice. He asked a series of closed questions which I recognized as background questions used to qualify me as a prospective client. He then asked a few more in-depth questions including:

- Do you use an investment advisor now?
- Who do you use?
- Are you satisfied?

I said, "I appreciate your prospecting efforts. I have a cousin who is a vice president at a big brokerage firm, so I don't want to waste your time." I wanted to encourage him in his sales efforts, but at the same time I did not perceive a need to do business with him. I did not think I had any Need POW that he could satisfy. Up to this point, our conversation had been pleasant and brief. My professional curiosity on his sales approach had been satisfied. He now knew that I had a relative providing the same service he wanted to offer. I was ready to resume work on my to-do list.

Then he recited my home address and demanded, "This is your home address, is it not?" This question in a demanding tone from a stranger made me feel uncomfortable. From my perspective—my perspective was the one that mattered most because I was the prospective customer—this question crossed over into inappropriate territory. In the security-conscious world in which we now live, I felt uncomfortable with a stranger telling me my home address and then asking me to verify it.

In addition to his inappropriate question, his tone came across like that of a police officer asking to see my driver's license. I was now sorry that I had answered the phone. He wanted to send literature and his business card to me. Since he had not discovered any

Need POW for me, his desire to send literature presented no value to me. I just did not want to be pestered again by a stranger.

You need to be able to sense when a relationship has progressed to the point where certain questions become appropriate to ask. Relationship is usually what determines whether a question is deemed appropriate or inappropriate. The way we ask questions, the tone of voice we use, our body language, the way we dress, and many other factors all combine to determine how questions will be received and answered.

I heard a comedian take sad and serious music from one song and combine it with silly lyrics from another song. By singing the words from a funny song while playing the music from a serious song, he created a discordant mess that was funny for a few seconds. After that it became confusing and almost painful.

Try to match the words you say with a tone of voice and body language that enhance and support your message. Often you convey even more through your body language and tone than with the specific words you use.

I once watched a childhood friend who is now a very successful attorney try a civil case before a jury. In his opening argument, my friend humbled himself by revealing aspects of his life with which most of the prospective jurors could identify. He seemed to have found something that he had in common with these people and made a connection.

As the trial progressed over the next week and a half, my friend presented his client's case by asking questions of a series of witnesses. He did not actually tell anyone anything. He made no statements or assertions, and yet he related an entire story simply by asking a series of insightful questions. He used humor, empathy, appropriate body language, and likable tone of voice and demeanor to elicit answers to his easily delivered questions. The questions asked and answers given painted a remarkably vivid picture of events that had trans-pired leading up to this trial.

My friend had a clear objective as he began questioning wit-nesses. He had prepared a list of initial questions to ask each witness, but he listened thoughtfully to the answers given in order to quickly determine the next question to ask. He let the jurors form their own conclusions to questions and their corresponding answers. The jury then went on to decide in his client's favor. What struck me as most significant in this trial process was that he convinced—or sold—twelve people to make a decision in his client's favor without making any statements and without telling them what to believe. All he did was ask questions.

Questions can be much more powerful than statements to influ-ence customers' perceptions of product, service, and price. It is much more effective when you allow customers to reach their own conclusion as they examine an issue than it is for you to tell them what they ought to think.

Using Questions to Position and Bracket

In my sales workshops and seminars, I like to conduct an exercise to demonstrate the incredible power the questions asked by sales professionals have to influence people's perceptions. We separate participants into two groups and give each group a true or false ques-tion. People in the two groups do not realize that each group has received a slightly different question.

The question for group one: The distance from Earth to the star Alpha Centauri C is less than five hundred light years. True or false?

The question for group two: The distance from Earth to the star Alpha Centauri C is less than five light years. True or false?

Then we ask both groups the same question: What is the distance from Earth to the star Alpha Centauri C? Invariably, the answers from people in group one hover around five hundred light years, while the answers from people in group two are much closer to the correct answer, about four light years. The discussion that ensues is usually lively, as participants try to determine why their groups answered so differently. When they realize that the initial question each group received was different, they understand how powerful questions can be to position or bracket ideas.

Skilled sales professionals recognize that they are selling as they proceed through the Ask phase of the selling process, just as they are when they present benefits in the Benefits phase, and just as they are when they close or ask for commitment in the Commitment phase. The questions you ask have a significant impact on the outcome of the selling process.

Questions can also bracket a potential future sales negotiation. For example, "Do you place orders with less than ninety days' lead time?" This question paints a picture of lead-time expectations. It might be natural for a negotiation of lead time to start at ninety days as a reference point following this question.

***

A subset of the Ask phase includes preparing for the sales conversation or sales call. This is usually done after you have qualified a prospective new customer who probably has a need, problem, opportunity, or want that you can satisfy. Additionally, you should have already determined that the prospective new customer is creditworthy and is someone with whom you want to do business. The call-preparation steps include:

1) Formulate a clear and realistic objective for the sales conversation in advance.

2) Use this clearly stated objective to plan the specific series of questions you will ask in the search for Need POW.

3) Write down the questions you plan to ask. You may not use the list during the call, but writing them down guides your thought process during call preparation.

The call objective depends on circumstances. If the product or service you offer can usually be sold in one sales call, then getting a first order might be a realistic objective for the first call. Most major sales require numerous calls before the first order is received, however. In this case, getting an order on the first call might not be a realistic objective. Examples of just a few of the many potential objectives for a first call might include:

- Getting an order
- Getting a contract signed
- Getting the agreement to do business when a need arises
- Getting the name(s) of the real decision maker(s)
- Establishing a business relationship as the foundation for doing business together
- Getting a second appointment to advance the sale to a higher objective.

CHAPTER SUMMARY

- *Recognize that the way questions are asked significantly influences the relationship.*

- *Understand that this is a conversation, not an interrogation.*

- *Know that questions have more power to influence than statements.*

- *Remember that questions can be used to position and bracket.*

- *Prepare for calls by writing a call objective and a corresponding list of questions to ask.*

CHAPTER 9

Benefits

THE GOAL OF the Benefits phase of the selling process is to connect the product or service you sell to the customer's expressed needs, problems, opportunities, or wants. This phase encompasses the expected sales presentation mode, which most participants consider classic selling mode. This is where you offer a solution to the customer's problem or need.

The most frequent challenge associated with the Benefits phase is the tendency of many sales professionals to leap into presenting benefits at inappropriate times, before the customer expresses his or her needs. Most salespeople are inclined to try solving problems before the problems are fully understood and developed. This simply leads to objections from the customer.

Timing and successful completion of the Ask phase are paramount in order to successfully present the Benefits phase. After your customer states his or her need and you have helped to develop its implications, then you can present the benefits in the following manner:

- Describe the value your product or service brings to the customer.
- Connect the benefits of your product or service to the customer's expressed need.

As the Benefits phase begins, consider the work you have already accomplished. You have laid most of the necessary foundation to sell your product or service in the Ask phase, and the customer has actually stated his or her need. You have developed that need with further discussion so that both you and your customer understand and agree on the need.

Defining Features and Benefits

What is a feature of a product or service? Features are facts and characteristics that describe a product or service. Examples of features include service lead time, service description, price, and product specifications such as size, shape, color, and weight. For example, a surf shop owner selling surfboards tells her customer, "This surfboard is ten feet long." She has just stated a feature of the surfboard. She has described something about the surfboard.

What is a benefit of a product or service? A benefit is the value of a feature to the customer. A benefit is what a feature will do for or means to the customer.

Beauty is in the eye of the beholder; benefits are in the eye of the customer. Only your customer can make it possible for you to transform a feature into a benefit. If the customer does not see any value in a feature, then it remains only a feature. To change a frog into a handsome prince, you have to find a princess who will kiss the frog. If you want to change a feature into a benefit, you have to find a customer who will see the value of the feature.

Using the previous example of selling a surfboard by stating the feature that it is ten feet long, a genuine benefit cannot be presented until the customer expresses a need. No doubt the surf shop owner previously conducted the Ask phase, and it went something like this:

> Owner: "Where do you surf?" (This is a background question.)
> Customer: "Along the Texas Gulf Coast."

> Owner: "What size waves do you usually ride there?"
> Customer: "The waves are usually relatively small, two to five feet high."

> Owner: "What is your biggest challenge surfing there?" (This is a Need POW question.)
> Customer: "Catching these small waves can be difficult. I have to paddle hard and fast and stay just inside the lineup where the waves are almost already breaking in order to catch them. I need to be able to catch these small waves easier."

From these answers, the surf shop owner knows that her customer's need is to catch waves more easily. She and the customer both know that his problem is a difficulty in catching small waves. He wants to catch these waves without having to paddle so hard and fast and without having to remain close inside the breaking zone.

With this expressed need, the surf shop owner can now transform a feature into a benefit.

Feature: ten-foot length → Benefit: easier to catch waves

She can present a true benefit by saying, "This surfboard allows you to catch small waves easily because of its long surface area and buoyancy." This statement points out the value of the ten-foot length to the customer.

If the customer had not expressed his need to catch waves more easily, the fact that the surfboard is ten feet long would not mean much to him. The customer might not have cared how long the surfboard is until the shop owner presented this benefit.

Focus on Benefits, Not Features

Features merely describe. Benefits sell.

It is frustrating and aggravating for a customer when a salesperson presumes that the customer will be charmed with the recitation of fifty features regarding a product or service. Who wants to be on the receiving end of this? Features are frequently devoid of all meaning to most customers.

When it comes to features, more is not necessarily better. Listing too many features may position your product or service as unnecessarily expensive. Present information that is appropriate, beneficial, and specific.

Information Overload

Accessing information today can be like trying to drink from a gushing fire hose. We absolutely need the water to stay alive, but the force of the torrent can obliterate us if we stand right in front of the hose. The most productive and effective salespeople quickly sift through the raging torrent of information available to them and efficiently glean the knowledge that is truly beneficial to them, their job performance, and their organizations. Yes, information is power, but too much of anything is poison.

In an average work day, most of today's sales professionals, purchasing professionals, and business people are deluged with information and requests in unmanageable quantities and modes: social networking, e-mail messages, regular mail, phone calls on an office line, cell phone calls (sometimes on multiple cellular devices), voice mail messages (many times on multiple systems), countless text messages, faxes, newspapers (either electronic or paper), periodicals, industry trade journals, blogs, and more. This could be doubled in their personal lives as work life encroaches into home life.

The expression *information is power* should be amended. *Useful information* delivered precisely at the time needed is power. Extraneous information delivered continuously is simply distracting.

This is where you as a skilled sales professional can provide great value to customers. Help your customers drink from the information stream without getting washed away. Provide the information needed to achieve their goals without either you or your customers wasting time sifting through irrelevant, nonessential trivia.

Objections

Remember the hypothetical story from part I of this book about the doctor who tried to prescribe surgery and medication without ever diagnosing a specific medical problem? The doctor bragged about the relatively short recovery time from his new and improved surgical technique and fewer side effects from the new drugs. He was presenting what he thought were benefits of the surgery and medication, but in reality these were only features. They were features with no clear benefits to the patient/customer. The result in this story was that the customer would object to what the doctor presented and probably would vow never to see this doctor again.

Presenting potential benefits before a need is stated by the customer frequently results in an objection rather than a sale. Trying to present benefits without expressed needs is one of the most common mistakes made by salespeople. Don't figuratively write prescriptions or schedule surgery for your customers before you and they recognize, understand, and agree on the correct diagnosis.

It can be difficult to resist the urge to jump in too early with a benefits statement. You can be so eager to help and so focused on the product or service you offer that you jump ahead to what you think is the only solution to what you initially perceive as a customer's problem. This tendency to offer solutions first and define problems second is very common among sales professionals. It is also very costly because many sales are lost due to this tendency.

Years ago as a new and relatively inexperienced sales representative, I was making an introductory call on a potential customer. The products I was selling were temporarily in very short supply throughout the industry. Through prospecting efforts, I became aware of a small toy manufacturing company that used the type of products that I was selling as raw materials for the toys it made. I scheduled an appointment with the purchasing manager. My call objective was to gather qualifying information on the company's raw material requirements as follows:

1) Which raw materials the company purchased
2) In what quantities
3) From which suppliers
4) For what prices

I planned to use this information to determine which of my products I should offer the prospective customer and at what prices as soon as my company had the extra supply to take on new business. If I achieved my objectives in this call, I would at least keep my potential new-business development pipeline full so that I would be ready when supply became available. I would be keeping the iron warm for future sales.

I arrived at the appointed time and signed in with the reception-ist. As I waited in the lobby, the serious, somber mood and corpo-rate culture of this company seemed at odds with what I expected for a toy manufacturer. The smiles, laughter, and joy that I would expect the company's products to elicit from its young customers were absent from the premises this morning.

When the purchasing manager opened the door to the lobby, I introduced myself and smiled. He did not respond in kind but ush-ered me into a large conference room. The two of us sat across from each other at a long conference table while the other fourteen chairs remained unoccupied. Only the lights above our two seats were illu-minated. The rest of the room languished in shadow.

He was not rude but merely acquiesced to brief introductory conversation. I asked questions to confirm that he bought the types of products I sold. His answers confirmed that they did purchase raw materials similar to those that I sold but at quantities barely reaching the minimum threshold that my company could economi-cally supply. I explained that we did not currently have enough sup-ply to take on new business but that I was interested in him and his company. I added that as soon as supply improved, I would like to offer my products to him as an alternate source. Then I began to present an industry update that used publicly available information to summarize market conditions and industry production capacity. I included information about current manufacturers of the types of raw materials he purchased, their plant locations, and their specific production capacities, and concluding with an emphasis on my com-pany's strengths and its position as a leader in the industry. Most of my customers appreciated this type of information. I presumed that this prospect would too.

Halfway through my ten-minute presentation, an attractive woman in her late twenties or early thirties entered the conference room. I paused briefly and greeted her. Like her coworker, she did not reply in kind but directed me to continue. Instead of sitting in a chair, she perched at the end of the conference table almost directly between me and the purchasing manager, her arms folded across her chest. I had to look around her to make eye contact with the purchasing manager. She told me to continue my presentation.

The woman's odd behavior and posture were distracting, but I did as she said and continued my presentation, concluding with a description of how my company was managing tight supply and high demand with sales control. We were not in a position to immediately take on new business, but we were preparing for the day when we could do so. Without any introduction, she then chastised me harshly, saying, "If you don't have any product to sell today, why are you even here?" Raising her voice and becoming very unpleasant, she said that I was wasting their time.

I told her that I was on her side and implied that I did not want an adversarial relationship. She replied that we were natural adversaries: I was selling and she was buying. We mutually concluded the meeting, and I left wondering what had happened.

What had gone wrong? I had achieved my information-gathering call objectives, but I certainly did not feel like this potential new customer's business was ready for me to bring in as soon as supply became available. I was distressed that a potential new customer would view me as an adversary simply because I was selling and she was buying. I drove away perplexed and troubled, trying to understand why I had encountered such hostility.

I can now review this disturbing memory through the lenses of experience and understanding to comprehend what happened and to plan an improved course of action should I find myself in similar circumstances in the future.

After conducting well over eight thousand customer visits and sales conversations, the lessons learned from the few sales calls that went spectacularly wrong and from the many that went wonderfully well are the most memorable. The most significant value of each of these sales experiences is to learn from them, and to emerge with greater skill and ability for application to future endeavors. This particular call was quite valuable, although it was very unpleasant at the time. The experience reinforced that relationship must always be the first priority. I had just begun to establish an introductory business relationship with the subdued purchasing manager. I had absolutely no relationship with the woman who crashed our meeting and behaved inappropriately. I was a stranger to them both, and they viewed strangers with skepticism.

From a social dynamics perspective, I should have stopped my presentation as soon as the woman entered the conference room. Since she did not respond when I introduced myself, I should have asked for her name and position. I should have invested a few minutes of time in an effort to get to know her. If I had been presenting to a large group of people, stopping the presentation would have been inappropriate. For an audience of one or two, stopping for this introduction would have been acceptable.

When the woman initially crashed our meeting, I had an intuitive feeling that she might be the owner of the company. I should have trusted my intuition by confirming her position and then asking questions to discover the problems she faced.

Through the lens of the ABCs of the professional selling process, I can now see that I should have stopped my presentation to ask questions. I would have discovered what was most important to this customer; and, most important to me, I would have determined who the real decision maker was. I later learned that this prospective new customer's existing supplier of raw materials could not supply all of the company's raw materials requirements. The purchasing manager and the woman were upset with their existing supplier (my competitor) and the industry-wide shortage of raw materials. They vented their frustration on me.

I thought they would value my industry-update presentation, but they had not expressed their needs to me. Therefore, my presentation was merely filled with features, not benefits. This simply produced objections.

As the woman crashed my meeting with the purchasing manager, intuition whispered in my mind that she probably owned the company. I later determined that my intuition was correct. The woman was in fact the new owner of the company.

After this sales call, I learned that she had just inherited the company and was probably scrambling to learn the business. She was very upset that her existing supplier could not supply all the raw materials she needed to run her business. It is possible that she also might have been grieving over the loss of the relative from whom she inherited the company. She took her frustration out on me after my presentation. I could have uncovered these problems that I intuitively suspected, listened to and acknowledged her concerns as she vented, developed her need for raw materials, and followed up with an offer to try to expedite raw materials to her as soon as supply allowed.

Trying to present benefits without first discovering, revealing, and developing the implications of Need POW carries significant risks in the form of customer objections. This example also illustrates the interconnectedness of relationship with the ABCs of the professional selling process.

***

Objections that prevent a customer from buying a product or service may be stated or unstated by the customer and therefore known or unknown to you, the sales professional. Unstated objections are vexing and frustrating. How can you overcome an objection if you don't know what it is? Stated objections can at least be addressed and possibly overcome. Unstated objections must first be converted to stated objections before you can even begin to overcome them. Once an objection is created, it must be overcome or mitigated in order for the sale to proceed. As in most matters involving problems, prevention is better than cure.

I address objections in this section on the Benefits phase of the ABCs of professional selling because objections frequently surface when benefits are presented. Perhaps surprisingly, objections are usually created by those who fear them most: salespeople. How and why do salespeople create their own problems?

Objections usually arise because the salesperson has unwittingly made one or more mistakes in the selling process, typically presenting what he or she thinks are benefits without first learning the customer's needs. As stated previously, benefits cannot really exist without expressed needs; so the salesperson ends up presenting mere features with the false expectation that the customer is going to like them and want to buy.

If the customer does not perceive value from the presented features, the customer usually responds with an objection. A customer who tells the salesperson why he or she will not buy is providing a stated objection. A customer who leaves, ends the sales conversation, or simply does not buy is providing an unstated objection.

The concept that objections are the creation of unwitting salespeople may be difficult for some to initially accept. Consider the objections or disagreements we all encounter in everyday conversations. These statements of disagreement must follow some form of comment, assertion, claim, or remark. Otherwise, what is there to disagree about?

Similarly, a customer can only form an objection when there is something to object to. Whether the objection is stated or unstated, the sad result is that no sale is made unless the sales person overcomes the objection.

Most sales calls culminate in one of the following three results:

1) A sale

2) A continuance or advance toward a potential future sale

3) No sale, usually for one or more of the following reasons:

   a) *The customer objected to something but did not state the objection, so the sales professional did not know which objection to overcome.*

   b) *The customer did state the objection, but the sales professional could not overcome it.*

   c) *The sales professional failed to employ the ABCs of the professional selling process when he or she did not ask for the appropriate commitment after presenting benefits.*

Which of these two alternatives is preferable?

1) Catch a cold and someone offers a new medicine to cure it

2) Do not catch a cold in the first place

Objections are similar to colds; prevention is far preferable to cure. Skilled sales professionals prevent objections by refraining from any attempt to present benefits until a need is expressed by the customer.

No sales professional is perfect. Objections happen. (This might look good on a T-shirt.)

When a customer states an objection, skilled sales professionals frequently ask for clarification to make sure they really understand what the customer is objecting to. If the customer says nothing and does not agree to buy when you have just been talking about what you think are benefits, then it is likely that an unspoken objection exists. This would be a good time for you to ask a question such as, "Have I said something that you do not agree with? Please help me to understand." Usually you must convert unstated objections to stated objections to overcome them.

Objections frequently go unstated out of politeness; the customer does not want to offend the salesperson by saying no. This is more common in some cultures than others. Another reason for not stating an objection is apathy. The customer simply doesn't care. The salesperson has not discovered the customer's need.

If you sense that a customer is not expressing an objection out of politeness, try to put the customer at ease with humor or levity. Remember Tom Cruise's line in the movie *Jerry Maguire*: "Help me to help you"? Cruise's sports agent character repeated this line over and over to his client, a professional football player played by Cuba Gooding Jr. Skilled sales professionals let their customers know that both parties benefit when concerns are stated and discussed.

Once an objection is stated, attempt to overcome it with the following process:

1) Clarify it.

2) Clear up any misunderstandings that might exist.

3) If a solution to the objection exists, present the solution. Ask the customer if he or she is satisfied.

4) If the customer is satisfied and the objection is overcome, proceed with the rest of the ABCs of selling.

If you cannot overcome the customer's objection, the sale will not proceed. Recognize that even the greatest of sales professionals cannot overcome all objections. The product or service being sold can also trigger objections. You might not have a product or service to solve the customer's problem or fill the customer's need.

Intuition ("Use the Force, Luke")

To sense when a customer has an unstated objection, pay attention to all forms of communication the customer might be using, such as:

- What he or she says.
- How the customer says it: tone of voice, volume, word choice.
- Body language.
- Intuitive messages.

Sales professionals cannot read minds, but you can certainly observe evidence of minds at work and make meaningful inferences. For example, an illiterate person can hold a comic book in one hand and a chemistry textbook in the other and sense the difference. One is thin, lightweight, and contains funny drawings with few words, while the other is thick, heavy, and contains symbols, forms, and equations along with many words.

Tuning in to all forms of communication requires awareness, like using a floodlight to illuminate a wide area. When you find something of particular interest, focus your spotlight on it for greater understanding to help you avoid surprise objections that could be created in the dark.

You can discern more from intuition than you might realize. Go back to the example of a nonreader looking at a comic book and a chemistry book. The nonreader intuitively discerned that the comic book is intended to entertain and the chemistry book is intended to educate.

Observing the books attentively, the nonreader probably could discern whether the comic book is a brooding and introspective depiction of a dark superhero or a lighthearted and humorous take on school life and that the chemistry book is serious in nature and covers a technical, weighty topic in detail. Without the ability to read and understand a single word, the nonreader could glean the intent and feel of these books.

Similarly those of us who cannot read minds can still glean the intent, mood, and feel of another person's thoughts by attentively observing the manifestations of a mind at work. I do not know anyone who can read minds, but I do know people who can intuitively sense how other people feel and what other people care about. Skilled sales professionals do not ignore the communication that comes to them through intuition. Often intuitive insight comes in the softest of voices but carries the most profound and meaningful of messages.

Presenting Benefits

To reinforce a previous point, you should present benefits after your customer expresses Need POW. This is one of the few times in the selling process when you are encouraged to talk.

First consider how your product or service will address the customer's stated need. Determine exactly how the product or service will benefit your customer in one or more of the following ways:

- Satisfy the expressed need or want
- Solve the clearly understood problem
- Help the customer capitalize on a recognized opportunity

Next describe clearly, simply, and succinctly how your product or service will benefit the customer. This is frequently referred to as a benefits statement. Simply tell the customer how your product or service will satisfy the stated need. Focus on providing the solution to the need, not on the product or service itself. Skilled sales professionals recognize that a customer is buying the solution to a need, not merely a product or service.

Technical Knowledge and Expertise with Product or Service

Different products and services require different levels of technical knowledge, understanding, and expertise for you to sell them effectively. The Benefits phase of the selling process is the most critical phase for you to demonstrate this knowledge, understanding, and expertise. How can you formulate a clear benefits statement without first understanding what your product or service can do for the customer?

For most sales professionals, the biggest challenge in the ABCs of selling is to discover, develop, and understand the customer's need. Frequently the second biggest challenge is to apply your knowledge of the product or service to satisfy the customer's need.

For example, a pharmaceutical representative trying to get doctors to prescribe his or her products would need technical knowledge of how the medications ease symptoms of specific ailments or cure diseases in order to present appropriate benefits statements.

Sales professionals who are technically oriented tend to especially enjoy this part of the selling process. I know salespeople who have doctorate degrees in engineering and science. This technical expertise can be a tremendous asset if it is employed appropriately in the selling process. Sales professionals who possess superb technical knowledge and expertise in the beneficial applications of the products and services they sell bring added value to customers because they can easily understand how to satisfy their customers' needs.

Skilled sales professionals learn everything they can about their products or services with an emphasis on applications to satisfy customer needs. Detailed, accurate, and broad technical expertise of the offered products and services should include:

- How they are made
- How they work
- All of their features with a focus on application of features to become benefits to customers
- Options

As stated earlier in the book, beauty is in the eye of the beholder; benefits are in the eye of the customer. A word of caution to the technically minded: incorrect use of technical expertise can be just as damaging to the selling process as lack of technical expertise. It is easy for technically minded salespeople to go overboard as they discuss technical aspects of their product or service. I have watched salespeople annoy and offend customers by showing off their technical knowledge in an attempt to impress rather than to sell.

Cerebral showoffs are thinking only of themselves and are the only ones impressed by their acquired knowledge. Those who speak in technical jargon no one else understands, practice name-dropping, use acronyms and concepts unfamiliar to the customer, and simply try to impress with their intellectual prowess are miscalculating what the customer really wants. These frequent mistakes of the technically gifted salesperson are just as annoying as the shortcomings of the technically challenged one. The clueless salesperson with no knowledge of the product or service cannot effectively formulate a benefits statement, while the salesperson who is overly impressed with his or her own technical gifts does not know when to stop talking.

Regardless of your level of technical knowledge, the focus should be on addressing the customer's needs. If your customer is technically oriented or simply expresses interest in the inner workings of the product or service, indulge him or her with a technical feast as you present benefits. On the other hand, if your customer shows little interest in how the product works, stick to what the customer wants.

You should not be dismayed if you initially lack sufficient technical expertise. Desire can compensate for an initial shortcoming. Just dig in and learn everything you can about your product or service with the emphasis on applications to satisfy common customer needs. Take every training course available to you with this goal in mind. If your company employs a staff of researchers, scientists, and engineers, talk with them often and at length. Ask for help to understand the inner workings and applications of your product or service. The customer applications and problems you discuss with your company's researchers will help improve the products and services offered.

Often people who were virtually born with technical brilliance have a difficult time communicating technical matters to people who are not so technically inclined, although there are wonderful exceptions to this observation. This challenge in communicating may stem from the inability of the technically gifted to understand how someone else could not already know what is obvious to them.

On the other hand, people who initially struggle as they work diligently to understand a technical matter may actually have an advantage in presenting technical benefits to others. It is precisely because they have persevered to overcome an initial state of technical ignorance through careful study, deep questioning, and a focus on customer applications that they are able to empathize with someone who does not yet understand. This education driven by the salesperson's own desire to understand and to sell is what allows him or her to help customers trod the same path from not knowing to knowing, to move from frustration to aha!

As quoted previously, Dr. Barry Asmus, senior economist, professor, popular speaker, and author, wrote: "A professor is someone who can take something simple and make it complicated; a communicator is someone who can take something complicated and make it simple." When presenting benefits, communicators outsell professors almost every time.

CHAPTER SUMMARY

- *Benefits sell, features merely describe.*
- *A benefit is the value of a feature to the customer, what it will do for the customer.*
- *First discover your customer's Need POW by asking questions.*
- *Then develop the implications of Need POW with further questions and discussion.*
- *After the customer expresses Need POW and its implications are clearly understood and developed, present the benefits of your product or service as the answer to the customer's explicitly stated Need POW.*
- *It is better to prevent objections than to overcome them.*
- *If an objection is created or discovered, it must be overcome in order to make a sale.*
- *Technical knowledge of products or services helps you to formulate and present benefits to the customer.*

CHAPTER 10

Commitment

THE C IN the ABCs of professional selling stands for the Commitment phase, in which you work to obtain appropriate commitment from your customer. Most selling courses of the past focused on closing; therefore, it is natural to conclude that the C stands for closing. Closing has negative connotations, however.

Closing implies that the selling process is over, but the selling process is never really over when your goal is to achieve major sales and ongoing relationships. The initial sale and commitment should lead to continuing business and a lasting relationship.

Closing also conjures up images of pushy salespeople using manipulative gimmicks and techniques to coerce customers into buying something they don't really want or need. Remember the story of the vacation time-share closer barring the way to the exit after a tropical breakfast at a plush Mexican beach resort? What customer wants to be closed? I joke sometimes with my customers that my boss and I use the good cop/bad cop routine: they better buy from me now or I'll bring in the hammer, my boss, to close them hard and close them fast. They laugh because they have seen this routine before—but not from me.

Professional buyers recognize cheesy closing techniques. These buyers have taken the training courses and experienced all the gimmicks. They are turned off immediately when a salesperson tries to use a spiffy, sure-fire technique to close them on something they do not want to buy. Salespeople who rely on coercive gimmicks are frequently relegated to the domain of small, one-time sales. Customers will see them coming and avoid them.

Many traditional sales training courses taught people to use a variety of techniques to close sales with customers. Graduates of these courses learned to close early, hard, fast, and often. Hammer the sale home. Don't let the big one get away. The primary shortcoming of this type of training is that it teaches salespeople to treat customers in demeaning, disrespectful, and condescending fashion. Customers became mere prey to be closed, like getting a fish into a net.

Many salespeople grew nervous every time they reached the point in the selling process when they were expected to close the sale. Their palms dripped with perspiration; they found it difficult to look a customer in the eye; their voices began to crack. These salespeople felt uncomfortable because they were expected to do something unpalatable, to treat their own customers in a disrespectful way. The process of closing tended to make them feel spurious. Could these feelings be hidden from their customers? That is unlikely.

This anxiety surrounding closing is an indication that something is missing – something isn't right. Commitment, on the other hand, is right. Commitment is similar to the word truth. Everyone respects it, although some may fear it. Commitment implies that the sales professional and the customer will be true to each other.

Contrast this implication to the previous connotation of closing: one party closing the sale on the other party.

Commitment conveys caring and concern. Commitment entails perseverance and strength. Commitment is nothing to be embarrassed about; it is something to seek with honor and confidence.

Asking for Commitment

Compared with traditional visions of closing, asking for commitment using the ABCs of professional selling is easy. Once you have laid the appropriate foundation for a sale with the Ask and Benefits phases of the process, commitment comes freely. The customer actually expects to commit when you request it following the Ask and Benefits phases and would be disappointed if you did not request it.

After you have presented benefits in response to your customer's expressed need, watch for buying signals from the customer. When you see, hear, or sense buying signals, ask for commitment.

Customers communicate their readiness to buy in any number of ways. They may comment that they agree with the benefits you have presented and understand how these benefits would satisfy their need. They might make comments such as, "Sounds good" or "Yes, that would be better" or "That would solve my problem." They might ask questions implying that they are considering placing an order, such as:

- What is the lead time for delivery?
- When can we start?
- What colors are available?
- What is your price for this product?
- Can I see your contract?

- What are your credit terms?
- What kind of technical support is available to me?
- How will you install this item?

Your customer may show readiness to commit with body language. The customer might lean forward in the chair, move to get a better view of your proposal or product, uncross his arms, or nod her head.

Which type of commitment to pursue depends on the circumstances. Major sales usually require more than seven sales calls and conversations with a wide variety of key decision makers at the company you are trying to sell to, many times over a period of months or even years. The type of commitment to pursue in each sales conversation depends on how far this sustained selling process has progressed.

If you are selling a product or service that does not require lengthy lead time to supply or buy it, then you might find it appropriate to go ahead and ask for an order. In response to your previously presented benefits statement, if the customer leans forward and says, "That sounds good," this is your cue to ask for commitment with requests such as:

- Would you like me to schedule delivery for you?
- When can we start?
- When would you like your first delivery?
- What quantity would you like delivered?

Once your customer has communicated acceptance with one or more buying signals, you can ask for commitment with confidence. Failing to ask for commitment now would be like a waiter tantalizing a diner with a dessert cart after a delicious meal and then refusing to take an order for blackberry cobbler with a scoop of vanilla ice cream. Skilled sales professionals don't disappoint their customers by not asking for commitment after their customers indicate agreement with the presented benefits.

The appropriate commitment you seek depends on the circumstances, the length and complexity of the selling process for your product or service, and your relationship with the customer. Regardless of the variety of circumstances, however, you should seek some type of commitment. Examples of commitment types for which you might ask include:

- An immediate order
- Agreement to sign a multiyear contract
- Agreement to engage services in the future when a project need develops
- An increase in supply position
- Agreement to buy other products and services
- Introduction to other decision makers
- A follow-up meeting to advance toward a future sale

Prepare by making a list of potential commitments to ask for as you plan your call. This is only a working list, however, because you may need to change which commitment to pursue depending on how your call goes. Many good sales professionals have made calls in which they planned to simply ask for commitment to schedule a future meeting to advance the sale as they developed a relationship with a new customer, only to receive unexpected buying signals during the call and end up asking for and receiving an initial order.

Ask for the most valuable commitment appropriate in your specific selling process and circumstance. Now is not the time to be shy. You have worked hard and smart to get to this point. Don't disappoint your customer by not asking for the expected appropriate commitment.

***

Monsignor J. P. O'Sullivan, a priest filled with the wisdom of age, experience, and peace, once told me a story from his youth in Ireland. Prior to becoming a priest, he played in the world hurling championship in a stadium filled to capacity with many thousands of cheering fans. He received the ball directly in front of the goal, took the shot expected by his teammates and the crowd of spectators, and watched in agony as the ball sailed just over the crossbar, missing the goal by inches.

A half century later, the monsignor still heard the collective groan from the crowd, saw the disappointment in the eyes of his teammates, and felt himself blush with embarrassment. However, imagine how he would have felt if he had not taken the shot that was expected of him. The agony of failing to fulfill his commitment as a forward for his team would have been far worse than trying for the goal and missing. He did get more shooting opportunities later in the game, continued to keep his commitments by shooting when appropriate, and his team became the world hurling champions.

Failing to ask for appropriate commitment from your customer after presenting benefits and sensing buying signals is worse than being told no.

Every now and then a customer may ask *you* for commitment. When you have done remarkably well with the Ask and Benefits phases, the customer may ask you for commitment with questions such as:

- How do I place an order?
- Can we sign a contract now?
- How soon can we start?

These good things do happen with proper execution of the Ask and Benefits phases, but don't make a habit of waiting for your customers to ask you for commitment.

Asking for appropriate commitment is easy if you have properly established a foundation for major sales during the Ask and Benefits phases and established common ground for doing business with your customer in a good relationship. Not asking for commitment is the biggest impediment to getting commitment. If you don't ask, it is unlikely that you shall receive. Whose fault is this? It is your responsibility to ask for commitment.

If, however, you know your product or service will not satisfy your customer's need, it would be an understatement to call this an impediment toward getting commitment to doing business together. If you do not have a solution to your customer's need, you cannot present benefits; however, many times this situation will not be permanent. The only constant in the business world is change. If you have properly qualified the customer and he or she has the potential to need or buy the product or service you sell, then the commitment to ask for might be to keep in touch as the environment changes.

Another possibility would be to develop a product or service that will satisfy the customer's need. After all, necessity is the mother of invention. This could be the best thing that happens to your company if it leads to new and more profitable products or services.

Final Thoughts on Commitment

The traditional selling courses of the past put disproportionate emphasis on closing, but only moderate importance on the aspects of the Ask and Benefits phases described in this book. This top-heavy focus on closing sales put unnecessary stress and burdens on what was viewed as the end of the selling process. It was akin to laying a weak foundation, adding hurriedly and flimsily constructed walls, and then putting a crushingly heavy roof on top. Of course the structure had difficulty supporting the imposing roof.

If you take the time to build a solid foundation (relationship) followed by sturdy walls and structure (Ask and Benefits phases), then adding the roof (Commitment phase) will be much easier and the commitment longer-lasting. Best of all, the entire sales process will be less stressful.

CHAPTER SUMMARY

- *When the customer gives you a buying signal after you have presented benefits to fulfill an expressly stated Need POW, ask for appropriate commitment.*

- *When you have executed the ABCs of the selling process well, asking for commitment is easy and fun.*

- *Don't fail by failing to ask for commitment.*

CHAPTER 11

Putting It All Together

HERE IS A five-point summary of the ABCs of the professional selling process divided among three time frames.

At All Times

1) Focus on developing good relationships with customers as the foundation for doing business together.

Before Each Sales Call

2) Prepare by answering these questions:

   a) *What is your call objective?*

   b) *What questions do you plan to ask to discover and develop Need POW?*

   c) *What commitments could you seek?*

During Sales Calls

3) Ask. Be sure to ask questions directed toward discovering and developing Need POW.

4) Benefits. After your customer expresses Need POW, present benefits to connect your product or service to the fulfillment and satisfaction of the need.

5) Commitment. When the customer agrees with the presentation of benefits or gives a buying signal, ask for appropriate commitment.

As you apply this simple, effective, and principle-based process to make major sales, it is important for you to use your own style and strengths to make it your own. Everyone has certain unique talents and gifts; everyone has something he or she does better than anyone else. Skilled sales professionals capitalize on their strengths as they practice this process.

In his book *The Tiny Warrior,* author D. J. Eagle Bear Vanas wrote that we will achieve true happiness when we align what we do best with our life path. Many people spend so much time trying to overcome their weaknesses that they miss opportunities to build on their strengths. The most successful sales professionals incorporate their talents, strengths, and the things they like to do best in their approach to making major sales.

Successful sales professionals tend to be strong goal-setters and eternal optimists. They enjoy life and all the people around them. These individuals know that while others may not remember exactly what they say, the other people will remember how they made them feel. Successful sales professionals go out of their way to make people feel good. They want the people they meet with to be truly happier for interacting with them.

These successful sales professionals set goals with their specific strengths as the foundation. They then establish daily patterns to help them achieve those goals. This is a superb example to follow. As Aristotle wrote, "We are what we repeatedly do."

At the end of each day, sales professionals can ask themselves, "If I do the kinds of things I did today every day, will I be likely to achieve my goals?" If the answer is yes, they sleep well and peacefully. If the answer is no, they still try to sleep well and peacefully, but tomorrow they change their patterns so the answer tomorrow night will be a satisfying yesssssss!

Many times the sales you realize today are the result of the work you did every day for the past six months. The sales you will realize several months in the future will be the result of things you did today. Results do not come instantly; results come from sustained patterns of perseverance and dedication. It is important to make these patterns joyful, fulfilling, and relevant. Everyone yearns to be relevant.

Consider the encouraging words spoken by President Theodore Roosevelt in 1910:

> It is not the critic who counts, nor the man who points how the strong man stumbled or where the doer of deeds could have done them better. The credit belongs to the man who is actually in the arena; whose face is marred by dust and sweat and blood; who strives valiantly; who knows the great enthusiasms, the great devotions and spends himself in a worthy cause; who, at best, knows the triumph of high achievement; and who, at the worst, if he fails, at least fails while daring greatly, so that his place shall never be with those cold and timid souls who know neither victory nor defeat.

Great sales professionals must venture into the arena. They do it joyfully and with zest. All sales professionals occasionally experience defeat, but successful sales professionals learn from these experiences, know that these circumstances are temporary, and grow vigorously from them. Like bodybuilders exhausted from strenuous workouts, they advance stronger and more capable with each sales experience.

Best wishes for great success to you and your customers.

Epilogue

I EXITED THE lobby of Elite Products Company and walked to my car, replaying my brief conversation with the purchasing agent, Erica Hildebrand. Could it be called a conversation? How many words had to be said in order to call it a conversation? What could I have done differently? What outcome had I really expected? Had I really considered in advance exactly what outcome I wanted? Surely this was not it.

The face of the young man in the lobby who seemed to empathize with my embarrassment resonated in my mind. I again saw the name on his badge in my memory: Steve Link. I wondered what role he played at Elite Products. When I returned to my office, I called Sandy Mercer, a market development specialist in my company's technical services group. Her job was to focus on how our products could be applied to solve technical problems in specific customer applications. "Sandy, I remember you telling me that you met several people from Elite Products Company last year at the industry trade show on the West Coast. Does the name Steve Link ring a bell with you?"

"Yeah, Steve was there. His father is president and majority stockholder. Let me pull Steve's card...OK, he's the business development manager. As I recall, he mainly comes up with new products."

I described to Sandy my most recent visit to the company and then thanked her. This background information on Steve would be very helpful.

The next day I called Elite Products Company. "Elite Products," answered a voice that sounded like Leslie, the gatekeeper/receptionist.

"I'm calling for Steve Link," I said.

A moment later, I heard, "Steve Link here."

"Hi Steve. This is the guy you witnessed in your lobby yesterday conducting the world's shortest sales call."

A hearty, joyful laugh erupted over the phone. "Actually, I've seen sales calls with even fewer words exchanged with Erica."

"Steve, the reason that I'm calling is to ask for your perspective." I gave him my name and the name of my company.

Steve quickly interjected, "I'm very familiar with your company and its extensive product line. I've spoken with several people from your technical support group at conferences."

"I understand that you are the business development manager at Elite, with a focus on developing new products. Is that correct?"

"Yeah, that's right."

"Would you like to join me for lunch next Wednesday? It would be helpful if I could get an understanding of what problems and challenges you are facing so that I might be able to offer potential solutions."

"Sure," Steve replied without hesitation.

On Wednesday of the following week, I picked up Steve at his office in my freshly washed and neatly vacuumed company car, a silver Chevrolet Impala. As we drove to Steve's choice of restaurants, Big Daddy's Pit Grill, we accelerated up the entrance ramp to the freeway to match unusually light traffic at 65 miles per hour. I noticed a police car ahead with lights flashing in the process of stopping a speeder. The police car stopped behind the now stationary speeder on the shoulder. As we passed on the left, the police officer was opening the door to his squad car with traffic whizzing by just inches away from him.

I commented, "Now there is a dangerous job."

Steve smiled. "You know, I have a friend from high school who just became a police officer. The crazy thing is that he never took anything seriously before, and none of us ever took him seriously either. He was the biggest goofball and jokester, lots of fun and a good buddy of mine. I still can't believe anyone else will take him seriously as a policeman. I met him for dinner last week. He was still in his uniform right after his shift. As we sat at our table, a lady walked by, looked at him respectfully, and greeted him, 'Hello officer.' He immediately replied in a deep, robotic voice, 'Hello citizen.' When he sees people doing something good, and when they call him officer, he loves to call them citizen!" Steve laughed again.

I smiled at Steve's story. The sound of his laughter and the light-hearted joy he exuded was a welcome comfort to me. I genuinely enjoyed his company. As we ordered lunch, I said, "Steve, I recognize that no one buys a product unless it satisfies a specific need or solves a particular problem. I want to find out what you, Erica, and your team at Elite Products need or what problems you may be having, so that I might be able to offer something of value to help. But as you witnessed the other day, I'm having difficulty even establishing any meaningful dialogue that would allow me to ask the questions I need to ask."

Steve responded, "Look, I'll be glad to talk with you and offer advice. I'm a salesman at heart, and I suspect that your company does have something that could help us with future products and maybe even some existing products. However, I won't interfere with Erica and our purchasing group and their role buying raw materials for our company. I will not tell them what to do, what products to buy, or who to buy them from. That's up to Erica."

"As it should be. I understand, and your advice to help me determine what Elite Products Company needs would be truly appreciated."

Steve continued, "Erica is under pressure from her boss to reduce raw materials costs for our plant. Everybody and his brother want to sell her their stuff. She is busy keeping the plant stocked with raw materials, under pressure to reduce costs, and does not have time to see every salesperson that constantly calls her requesting meetings."

Our server delivered a cheeseburger for Steve and a chicken enchilada plate for me. The discussion continued as we enjoyed our meal.

"Steve, what are your major challenges now as you work to develop new products for Elite?"

"Well, as you already know, we have a fairly broad product line being sold globally through well-established retail outlets. Our biggest concern is the latest pending environmental regulation set to become enforceable just eleven months from now." Steve cited the name of the looming legislation. "This rule will require us to either reformulate our biggest-selling product to comply, or we will be forced to discontinue making our biggest-selling and most profitable product. This serious threat has our entire company focused on saving our existing, mature product. This defensive but necessary focus forces me to temporarily put our new-product development on hold."

"I'm familiar with the pending regulation. My technical services group is well versed on this topic. How do you plan to respond?"

Steve's brow furrowed and his smile disappeared. "We need to replace the primary component in our product with a material that would not be classified as a volatile organic compound. So far, we do not have any alternate materials that will work in our existing formula. Our technical director, Louis Brannigan, and his staff of chemists are working feverishly in our lab on this project now."

"What would happen if they don't find a replacement in time?"

"I am completely confident that they will find something, but I don't know what it will be," Steve replied stoically. "If not, we will be forced to stop making our biggest-selling product."

I asked, "How much revenue and profit is at stake here?"

"That's proprietary information, but you could do the math with some amount of information available publicly on our product's sales volume to estimate that the impact on sales revenue would be over fifty million dollars per year."

"Steve, if I could offer a real solution to this fifty-million-per-year problem, would you help me to schedule an opportunity for my technical services group and me to discuss the solution with your team at Elite?"

"Yeah, I could get you in front of the key decision makers, but tell me what you have in mind first."

"My company makes a line of materials currently not classified as volatile organic compounds in consumer products because their vapor pressures are below the defining threshold and because they are nonreactive in the atmosphere. Some of them could be real candidates to replace your key ingredient that is the culprit to this regulation."

Steve seemed a bit relieved as he said, "I'll schedule a meeting in our lab with Louis Brannigan, Samantha Lopez, his chief chemist, Erica, and possibly several others."

"I'll include Sandy Mercer from my technical services group. This sounds like a great plan."

Three weeks later Sandy Mercer, the market development specialist in my company's technical services group, and I arrived for the meeting at Elite. As we entered a conference room adjacent to the laboratory, I was pleased to see the Elite team already seated at the table. I smiled and greeted Erica Hildebrand, the purchasing agent. She introduced Sandy and me to her boss, Janet Cruise, the purchasing director. Steve introduced us to Louis Brannigan and Samantha Lopez. The room grew loud with pleasant conversation as we got comfortable with each other and understood our respective roles and responsibilities.

Finally I began our discussion with a series of questions to further define the impact of the pending environmental regulation. We discussed our perceptions of what the regulation was intended to do, its consequences, and exactly what it meant to Elite Products Company. Sandy and I followed up with questions to quantify the impact in revenue for Elite Products.

Samantha admitted, "We will lose over fifty million dollars in sales per year unless we are able to find a nonvolatile organic compound that will still work in our formulation. We need one that will not compromise our product performance, and we need it within ten months from today."

Sandy and I used this expressly stated need as a cue to present the benefits of our product. Sandy presented the characteristics and applicable features of our product and described the value of its performance to Elite's formula. Our product was not classified as a volatile organic compound, therefore it would comply with the pending regulation.

"The benefit of our product to you is that you can use it to make your existing product comply with the pending environmental regulation and therefore continue generating large sales and revenue from your mature product," Sandy said.

We reviewed the product's chemical attributes and discussed the preliminary results of applications testing already done in our lab. Our potential replacement material would not cause any measurable drop in performance of Elite's product. Everybody in the room smiled.

Erica then asked, "How much does your product cost?"

From our knowledge of the market in which we competed, Sandy and I had a good idea of what Erica was paying for her current raw material, a raw material that would no longer be acceptable in ten months. We knew that the selling price of our product was at least 20 percent higher. Our product was synthetically produced and therefore more expensive to make. There was nothing that Sandy and I could do about the higher cost of production for our superior product. We were also aware that we had competitors who sold alternative products to our nonvolatile organic compound material. Although our product could theoretically be priced to capture more of its value to Elite Products, we needed to price our product to be competitive with our competitors' products. Otherwise, we would simply give our customer a reason to replace our product in the near future. I quoted our price that was at least 20 percent higher than the material Erica was currently buying.

As expected, Erica flinched. "That will cost us five hundred thousand dollars per year more than we are paying now," she exclaimed.

"Value equals benefits minus cost," I answered. "In this case, the benefit is preservation of fifty million in revenue. I realize that the profit margin associated with this amount of revenue is probably proprietary, so let's focus on the revenue number in this value equation. As you just mentioned, the additional cost associated with using our product instead of your existing raw material is five hundred thousand dollars. Plugging these numbers into the value equation, the benefit to Elite Products would be fifty million in preserved sales revenue minus the additional cost of five hundred thousand equals a value of over 49.5 million. Isn't this value worth discussing further?"

Louis preempted an expected response from Erica saying, "You have convinced me that your product warrants consideration. Please send us a one-gallon sample right away so that we can test it in our lab to determine how it might impact our product's performance."

Sandy gladly responded, "We'll send a sample via overnight courier."

After additional conversation to conclude this meeting, I asked, "Can all of you join Sandy and me for lunch?"

Erica, Samantha, and Steve accepted our invitation. Louis declined due to another meeting.

The five of us proceeded to Big Daddy's Pit Grill. As we entered the restaurant, the sound system seemed to be playing background music at a higher volume than during my previous lunch with Steve. David Bowie's voice sang "We can be heroes just for one day…" This mesmerizing melody continued with its synthesizer, heavy percussion, and bass.

Erica said, "David Bowie's 'Heroes' from the album of the same name!"

"You must be quite a David Bowie fan," I said.

"I sure am. I like all kinds of alternative rock, but Bowie is one of my favorites." Erica's voice was more animated than I had heard it before.

Our group's discussion over lunch flowed easily from business topics to family to things we all liked to do most. The conversation helped us feel comfortable working together on this material replacement project.

About three weeks later, I saw an advertisement for a David Bowie concert at the L.A. Forum. I dialed Erica's office phone number. Her voice mail greeting answered. After identifying myself and my company, I left this message, "Erica, would you and your husband like to join my wife and me for dinner and the David Bowie concert at the L.A. Forum?" I mentioned the date and suggested several restaurant ideas on where to meet in advance of the concert.

Later that day, my phone rang. "Terry, this is Erica. We would love to join you for the Bowie concert and dinner. That sounds terrific to me."

During the subsequent dinner and concert, my wife and I got to know Erica and her husband and enjoyed talking about a wide variety of interests and topics. We did not discuss business, but all of us became more at ease with each other.

The next time I called to schedule a meeting with Erica to follow up on our material replacement evaluation status, she agreed to meet with me on the requested date and time. When I arrived at the lobby and signed in with Leslie the receptionist, Erica appeared in the lobby before I even sat down to wait. "I have a conference room reserved for our meeting," Erica said as she offered me a cup of coffee on our way to the meeting room.

After some introductory conversation and discussion, I gave Erica an update on my company's applications laboratory tests being conducted by Sandy Mercer and my technical services team. I asked Erica, "What can you tell me about performance tests with our product in your lab?"

"Louis and Samantha tell me that performance tests are all good. We are ready to share our test results and discuss next steps."

Erica and I scheduled a follow-up meeting to include her technical staff and other key decision makers. Two weeks later, I arrived at Elite Products with Sandy Mercer for this follow up meeting.

We entered the same conference room adjacent to the laboratory. Sandy and I smiled as we greeted Erica, and the others. The mood permeating the room was noticeably more relaxed than in our initial meeting. As conversations ensued, a distinguished man with a stately appearance quietly entered the room. Graying, with neatly trimmed hair, wearing a white shirt and tie, he smiled and extended his hand. "Hi, I'm Frank Link," he said. I immediately recognized him from trade publication photographs. He was the president of Elite Products Company. He was also the father of my new friend, Steve Link.

"I'm very pleased to meet you, Mr. Link," I said as I told him my name. "This is Sandy Mercer, market development specialist from my technical services group."

The company president and Sandy shook hands as the president kindly remarked to us both, "Call me Frank."

Samantha Lopez, Elite's chief chemist, presented her performance test results of our product in the company's existing product formulation. Sandy presented similar results from our lab. All meeting participants were pleased that our substitute material performed as well as the existing material they would have to replace. Discussion continued without a hint of tension. I asked, "Does this mean that you have officially approved our material for use in your existing product formulation?"

"Yes, we have," said Louis Brannigan, the technical director. "We do not see any measurable performance difference."

"And since our material is not classified as a volatile organic compound, do you agree that it will allow your product formulation to comply with the pending environmental regulation?" I asked.

"Yes," Louis replied. "It will make us fully compliant. This is obviously a big relief and very good news. But we still need to run a full-scale plant trial with a full truckload of your product."

"I suggest the following action plan to bring this good news to fruition for you. Schedule the plant trial when convenient for you.

Place an order with us for the first full truck. If the plant trial is successful as we all expect it to be, future orders can be delivered in rail cars to achieve economies of scale. Erica and I can discuss pricing and contract terms and conditions so that we can document an agreement satisfactory to both our companies in advance of this first order. Would this plan meet your expectations?"

"Yes, that is exactly the course of action I planned to take," said Janet Cruise, the purchasing director. "Let's proceed as you suggest. We need to begin shipping the newly formulated and environmentally compliant product to our customers in advance of the pending regulation."

A few months later as I arrived for one of my periodic meetings with Erica, Louis, Samantha, Steve, and an expanding list of key contacts at Elite Products, I smiled as operators connected a hose to unload the fifth full rail car order of the material Elite was now buying from my company. Steve shook my hand in the lobby as we proceeded to his office. "Good job, citizen," he said with a broad smile. "Let's get busy talking about new products now."

To contact the author, please visit website:
www.TheHeartOfSelling.net

www.ingramcontent.com/pod-product-compliance
Lightning Source LLC
Chambersburg PA
CBHW051320170526
45166CB00002B/621